DELTA Business Communication Skills

Series editors
Susan Lowe and Louise Pile

Socialising

David King

PUBLISHING

DELTA Publishing
Quince Cottage
Hoe Lane
Peaslake
Surrey GU5 9SW
England

First published 2005

Critically read by Sarah Baldy-Kühnapfel
Edited by Catriona Watson-Brown
Designed by Caroline Johnston
Illustration by Phill Burrows
Cover design by Peter Bushell
Picture research by Suzanne Williams
Printed by Halstan and Co., Amersham, Bucks

Photo acknowledgments
Alamy *front cover*/ImageState/Pictor International,
p 8tr (Chris Fredriksson), 8cl (acestock); Getty Images
pp 8br (Thomas Barwick), 14 (Tobias Prasse),
20 (Christopher Bissell), 29 (Mel Yates), 32 (Juan
Silva), 33l (altrendo images); Punchstock *Royalty-free*
pp 8tl (Photodisc Red/Andersen Ross), 8cr (Digital
Vision/Flying Colours Ltd), 9 (PhotoAlto/Eric Audras),
15 (BananaStock), 21 (image100), 26 (PhotoAlto/Teo
Lannie), 33r (Stockbyte Platinum), 40 (Dynamic
Graphics Group / Creatas), 41 (Brand X Pictures/ER
Productions); Topfoto p 8bl (Novosti)

Photo editing: Pictureresearch.co.uk

ISBN 1-900783-94-0

Contents

Introduction

DELTA Business Communication Skills is a new series which uses a learner-centred approach to develop key communication and language skills essential for today's international business environment. The series is designed for learners of business English at pre-intermediate and intermediate level, either pre-service or in-service, and it can be used either in the classroom or for self-study.

Features of the series include:

- Individual Needs analysis and Learning journal
- Awareness-raising activities
- Extensive personalized exercises
- Tips for effective performance in business
- Helpful suggestions for language study
- Regular language reference and review sections
- Photocopiable resources
- An integrated audio CD
- Full transcripts and answer keys

Socialising aims to develop the skills and language needed to cope effectively in English in a range of typical social situations that business people might encounter, using a variety of means of communication. There are six core units, each containing:

- **Context** – to raise awareness of the skills and issues (including cultural aspects) involved in the various activities of socialising, and to introduce different strategies for developing these skills
- **Presentation** and **Practice** – of core language (vocabulary, functional phrases and pronunciation) linked to these skills
- **Tips** (cultural or language related) – on how to be more effective in social situations
- **Consolidation** – to allow learners to apply what they have learned to their own work situation
- **Reference** – useful phrases and vocabulary related to each unit
- **Review** – study suggestions and further practice (ideal for homework/self-study)

The book also contains:

- **Needs analysis**. This encourages you to consider what you need to focus on in order to get the most out of the book and your learning.
- **Learning journal**. This provides the opportunity to reflect and personalize what you have studied in the book.
- **Resources section**. This provides additional material such as photocopiable frameworks and cards.
- **Answer key**. This is designed to enable you to work either alone or with a teacher.
- **Transcripts**. These detail the content of the accompanying CD.

How to use this book

Step 1

It is recommended that you start by working through the **Needs analysis** (page 5). This will help you to:

- think about your strengths and weaknesses in socialising in English;
- identify and prioritize your immediate and future needs for socialising;
- determine the order in which you work through the core units of this book.

I hope you enjoy using this book.

D. King

David King
Author

Step 2

You should then familiarize yourself with the **Learning journal** (page 6), to which you are asked to refer at the end of every core unit.

Step 3

You should work through the units in the order they feel most appropriate to your needs and interests.

About the author

David King has extensive general and Business English teaching and teacher training experience. He has written and edited a range of print and multimedia language-learning materials.

Needs analysis

Business is primarily about people and how we get on with each other. Because of this, the activities of socialising play a major part in doing business. The success of a business deal can depend on how well we welcome a guest or on knowing the right thing to say at a business function.

So, what about you? What are your priorities when approaching the topic of socialising? Consider first who you need to socialise with in English for business. What social situations do you find yourself in at work, and how effective do you think you are in those situations?

1 **Tick (✔) the points below which are true for you.**

At work, I need to speak English when meeting and socialising with:

- clients ☐
- colleagues ☐
- high-status managers and associates ☐
- people who are working for me ☐
- project partners ☐
- suppliers ☐

At work, I meet and socialise with people in English:

- at conferences ☐
- at trade fairs ☐
- after business meetings ☐
- when meeting professional associates ☐
- when welcoming:
  - clients ☐
  - colleagues ☐
  - project partners ☐
  - suppliers ☐
- when visiting:
  - clients ☐
  - colleagues ☐
  - project partners ☐
  - suppliers ☐
- in work teams ☐
- at internal meetings ☐
- at work parties/social events ☐

2 **Each unit of this book focuses on a different area. Look through the summaries at the beginning of Units 1–6 and think about which areas you need to develop. Developing your awareness of what you already do well and what you could do better will allow you to focus on improving those skills you really need. Note down the units you intend to work through in order of priority for you – in terms of the area in which you feel you are weakest, or which is currently of most importance to you.**

Priority	Unit number and focus area
1	
2	
3	
4	
5	
6	

Before you start working through the units – starting with the one you listed as your top priority – look at the Learning journal on pages 6 and 7.

Learning journal

During the course
As you work through each unit, make a note of useful phrases and vocabulary you might use in real life. An example is given, but what you note down will depend on your own learning pattern.

Example

> **Unit:** 1
> **Useful language:**
> You must be (Marcella).
> You're based in … , aren't you?
> Sounds interesting
> **Useful tips:**
> Repeat a new name and use it in my conversation.

Your Learning journal

Unit: 1 **Useful language:** **Useful tips:**	**Unit:** 2 **Useful language:** **Useful tips:**
Unit: 3 **Useful language:** **Useful tips:**	**Unit:** 4 **Useful language:** **Useful tips:**
Unit: 5 **Useful language:** **Useful tips:**	**Unit:** 6 **Useful language:** **Useful tips:**

After the course

It is important to consolidate your learning, both during your course and afterwards at work. After you have completed each unit, you should decide how you will continue to develop your skills, e.g. which consolidation/revision exercises you will do or how you will practise what you have learned in the workplace. Note that it is helpful to give yourself realistic deadlines!

Make notes on developing your skills, for example using a framework like the one below. An example is given to help you.

Example

Unit: 3

Focus area: Building rapport

I need to:
build and maintain effective working relationships with project partners using English as our means of communication.

To do this better, I intend to:
concentrate on and practise useful phrases as in Unit 3 Practice (Exercises 1 and 2) – by end of May. I also need to develop my intonation and pronunciation skills as in Practice Exercise 3 and will do further intonation work as in the Study suggestion (June).

Your planner

Unit:

Focus area:

I need to:

To do this better, I intend to:

This book is designed to be used during and after a course, so keep it with you and refer back to it whenever you need to, and keep adding to your notes!

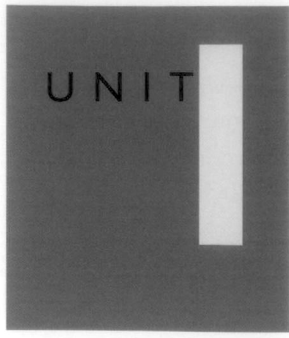

UNIT 1

Opening a conversation

THIS UNIT LOOKS AT:

- introducing yourself and other people and starting a conversation
- talking about jobs, products and companies
- welcoming people
- checking and clarifying what people say

Context | 1 **In what situations might you have to use English to introduce yourself and your company?**

2 **When meeting new people and starting a conversation in English, what do you find most difficult?**

- Knowing the correct language to use
- Knowing how to greet someone suitably: whether to shake hands, bow, exchange business cards, etc.
- Knowing how to address them after the introduction, for example, by first name or surname
- Knowing what to say to make the other person feel comfortable, to put him/her at ease.
- Understanding what the other person says
- Responding to the other person in the right way

Presentation

Lisa Stewart and Sean Howe work for a UK company called Speedsystems, based in Bristol. They are at a product launch to promote the company's new product range, called Choicemaster 3.

Introductions

1 🎧 **1.1 Listen to Lisa and Sean starting a conversation with a potential customer from another company. Underline the correct answers.**

1 <u>*Sean introduces Lisa*</u> / *Lisa introduces Sean* to the customer.

2 The customer *gives* / *doesn't give* them his business card.

3 Lisa repeats *the customer's name* / *the company's name* to check she has heard correctly.

4 Lisa *had heard* / *hadn't heard* of PD Solutions before.

5 The customer *had heard* / *hadn't heard* about Speedsystems before.

6 Speedsystems produces *office furniture* / *software*.

7 The customer works as *an engineer* / *a buyer*.

8 The customer is looking for a *faster* / *cheaper* system.

> **Tip** Introduce other people clearly and fully, with their full name and job title.

2 🎧 **1.1 There is one mistake in each of these extracts from the opening of the conversation. Listen again and correct each mistake.**

    It's

1 ~~I'm~~ Pedersen ... Henrik Pedersen.

2 I'm Sean Howe ... and here is my colleague Lisa Stewart ...

3 ... who's responsible to organizing the day.

4 I know. You're based in Stockholm, isn't it?

5 Your name's getting down.

6 ... and this new software you just brought out.

7 What sort of thing you looking for?

> **Tip** A good way to memorize a name is to repeat it and use it in your opening conversation.

Checking and clarifying

3 🎧 **1.1 Listen again and tick any of the following ways of checking and clarifying which you hear in the conversation.**

1 Could you say that again? ☐

2 Sorry, I didn't catch your name. ☐

3 Pardon? ☐

4 You're from ... which company? ☐

5 ... , aren't you? ☐

6 Sorry, I didn't quite get that. ☐

7 ... did you say? ☐

8 Sorry, what was that again? ☐

9 Could you repeat that for me? ☐

10 Is it? ☐

4 🎧 1.2 **Here are some more examples of opening conversations. Listen and complete each response.**

1 ▲ Hello, I'm Mr Cheng from Shanghai.

  ✦ Good morning, we've often _____ , but it's great to meet you _____ .

  ▲ Yes, I feel we _____ pretty well already.

2 ▲ I don't believe we've _____ .

  ✦ I'm Jill Anderson, Chief Buyer for Mayfield Productions. And you are ... ?

  ▲ Paola Cilento, from Gianni e Donna, Milan.

  ✦ Sorry, I _____ your first name – Paola, _____ ?

  ▲ Yes, Paola, Paola Cilento.

  ✦ Very pleased to meet you.

3 ▲ I'm so glad _____ . We've heard so many good things about you.

  ✦ It's a real pleasure to be here.

4 ▲ Good morning, Mr Nakita. I'm delighted you could come. _____ , Michael Evans.

  ✦ How do you do ... and what's your role in the project?

5 ▲ I'm terribly sorry, I'm sure we've met before, but _____ .

  ✦ Kate Price from Watership Publishing. We met at last year's conference in Madrid.

  ▲ Of course, nice to see you again.

Practice

1 **Put these words into the correct order to make complete sentences.**

1 Hello, / pleased to / Jill Davis / meet you. / my name's / and I'm really

2 Guy Cartier, / This is / Paris office. / in our / who works

3 our / introduce / Jean Paul Lemond, / Sales Manager. / Let me

4 you represent? / do / How do / What company / you do?

5 can't quite / I'm sure / before, / place you. / we've met / but I

6 welcome / I'd / you / like to / here today.

7 what / I didn't / you said. / quite catch / Sorry,

8 you could / so pleased / I'm / come.

9 for me? / but / Sorry, / repeat that / could you

10 you. / so pleased / to have / I'm / finally met

2 **Add a negative tag to the end of these sentences to make them into questions.**

Example You're representing Clayman Inc, <u>aren't you</u>?

1 Your company is based in Toulouse, _____ ?

2 You work with Michael Freeman, _____ ?

3 You've got a copy of our brochure, _____ ?

4 You're updating your product line, _____ ?

5 I believe you've already met Teresa Bellisario, _____ ?

6 You came to the conference last year, _____ ?

7 She works in the Milan office, _____ ?

8 I'm sure you'd like a coffee, _____ ?

3 1.3 **Listen to these greetings and underline the main stresses. Notice how quickly we say the unstressed words or parts of words.**

1 Pleased to meet you.

2 How do you do?

3 Sorry, I didn't catch your name.

4 I'm so glad you could come.

5 I'm really pleased we've finally met.

6 I'd like to welcome you here today.

4 1.4 **Listen to the same phrases broken down into 'chunks' (smaller parts) and repeat them.**

5 Use the cards on page 46 of the Resources section. Put them in a pile face down on the table. Pick up each card and use the word(s) in a sentence or question. If you're working with a partner, make up a short dialogue.

Example

┌ ─ ─ ─ ─ ─ ─ ┐
    do
└ ─ ─ ─ ─ ─ ─ ┘

▲ How do you do?

✦ How do you do? Did you have a good journey?

▲ Yes, fine, thanks, except for a short delay in Hong Kong.

6 Look at page 46 of the Resources section. Practise what you could say when meeting someone in these business situations.

Consolidation

1 How important is exchanging business cards in your business culture? What information is on your business card? Do people normally examine business cards carefully? How can exchanging cards be helpful when meeting new people?

2 Imagine that you are representing your company at a trade fair, conference or product launch. Prepare to introduce yourself, and to describe your job, your company and its products.

3 When you next meet someone for the first time, try out your ideas. Afterwards, think about how it went. What would you do differently next time?

➔ NOW TURN TO YOUR LEARNING JOURNAL AND MAKE NOTES ON THIS UNIT.

Reference

Useful phrases	*Vocabulary*

Useful phrases

Introductions

I'm / This is ...

How do you do?

Pleased/Delighted/Nice/Glad to meet you.

Let me introduce ...

You must be ...

Checking and clarifying

Could you say that again?

Sorry, I didn't catch your name.

Pardon?

You're from ... which company?

Sorry, I didn't quite get that. *

Sorry, (Peterson), did you say?

Sorry, what was that again? *

Could you repeat that for me?

Vocabulary

Talking about people

buyer

chief buyer

colleague

customer

engineer

sales manager

Talking about your company

to be based in

corporate training

office furniture

software

Talking about your product

concept

delay

draft

initial

to bring out

to come out

to get around

to speed up

turnaround

---

* informal

Study suggestion	Build up a bank of commonly used verb + preposition patterns. You can record these with a definition and an example:

Study suggestion

Build up a bank of commonly used verb + preposition patterns. You can record these with a definition and an example:

- by verb
  to get
  to get around = to spread: Your name's getting around.
  to get by = to survive: We got by with very little extra expenditure last month.

- by preposition
  out
  to bring out = to produce something new: Toyota have just brought out a new electric car.
  to come out = to be launched: Toyota's new car is coming out in the spring.

Review

Skills **When you meet someone for the first time, what sort of things can you say:**

1 to greet the person in a warm and welcoming manner?

2 to check and clarify what the other person says?

Useful phrases **Match the sentence beginnings (1–6) with the endings (a–f).**

1 How do	a aren't you?
2 You're based in Paris,	b don't you?
3 Delighted to	c introduce my colleague ...
4 You work for ICL,	d you do?
5 Let me	e a lot about you.
6 I've heard	f meet you at last.

Vocabulary **Complete each sentence with a preposition from the box.**

of around around out out in about up

1 We're bringing _____ a new version of the software next year.

2 Our aim is to reduce our turn_____ time to 48 hours.

3 We've heard a lot _____ you from your ex-colleagues.

4 I've heard _____ your company before.

5 I believe they're based _____ Munich.

6 Can you possibly speed _____ your delivery times?

7 You're becoming very well-known – your name's getting _____.

8 Our new product line came _____ in the spring.

Pronunciation I **Look at these dialogues. Mark the words you think are stressed and whether the intonation rises (↗), falls (↘) or rises and falls (↗↘). Read the conversations with the correct stress and intonation.**

1 ▲ I work for Oxford International.

　+ Oh, really? Which office?

2 ▲ I think you've already got the address of our website, haven't you?

　+ No, I haven't actually.

3 ▲ I think we've probably been involved in the same project.

　+ Oh, have we? When was that?

4 ▲ Hello, you must be Joachim, am I right?

　+ Yes, that's right. Pleased to meet you at last.

5 ▲ We're hoping to expand into Eastern Europe next year.

　+ Oh, are you? Tell me more.

6 ▲ I'm sure we've met before, but I can't quite place you.

　+ Have we? Maybe we met at the Madrid trade fair last year.

2 🎧 1.5 **Listen and check.**

UNIT 2

Making conversation

THIS UNIT LOOKS AT:

■ keeping a conversation going

■ showing interest and responding in a positive way to another person

■ turn-taking: making sure each person has an equal share of the conversation

■ talking about job roles, company plans and the business situation

Context

1 🎧 **2.1 Listen to these six dialogues. What are they about? Write the number of each dialogue next to one of these topics.**

job roles _____

company plans _____

a project _____

the general business situation _____

2 🎧 **2.1 The following descriptions match the dialogues. Listen again and write the number of each dialogue next to the correct description.**

☐ a company's plans for future growth

☐ a person's role in a project

☐ a person's area of expertise

☐ checking the details of a project

☐ forecasting the future

☐ a company's location plans

Presentation

Ricardo Castelli has just met Werner Klinsmann at Milan airport and is driving him to his hotel. Ricardo asks Werner about his job and company.

Talking about jobs and companies

1 🎧 **2.2 Listen to the first part of Ricardo and Werner's conversation. Tick T (true) or F (false) for each statement.**

	T	F
1 Werner's company has existed for only thirteen years.	☐	☐
2 Werner's company wants to extend its range of products.	☐	☐
3 Werner's job is to sell the company's existing products.	☐	☐
4 Werner's company is part of Rodux.	☐	☐
5 Werner's company has changed in the last two years.	☐	☐
6 Werner thinks his company is too old-fashioned.	☐	☐

> **Tip** Remember that your body language and eye contact are very important when making conversation.

2 🎧 **2.2 Listen to the opening of the conversation again. Complete the missing phrases.**

1 Can you _____ a bit more background to your company?

2 _____ for over 30 years now.

3 I see. So presumably that's _____ .

4 _____ look into new possibilities all over Europe.

5 You're part of a larger group, _____ ?

6 _____ a big investment in new technology.

7 Oh really? In _____ ?

8 _____ much more ready to respond ...

9 _____ positive ...

Continuing the conversation

3 🎧 **2.3 Ricardo continues the conversation by asking Werner's opinion about the business climate. Look at the dialogue below. Write each verb in the box in the correct place in the dialogue. Then listen to check your answers.**

> last   were   suppose   expected   make   sounds
> mirrors   creeping   look   mind   picking

Ricardo: [1]_____ really positive ... and how does the market [2]_____ to you at the moment?

Werner: Pretty good. Things [3]_____ a bit sluggish towards the end of last year, but I guess that's only to be [4]_____ , given world events. Orders have been [5]_____ up steadily since then, though, and overall, I [6]_____ we're cautiously optimistic. How about you?

Ricardo: Yes, that pretty well [7]_____ our own experience. [8]_____ you, I don't know how long this upward trend'll [9]_____ , with EU interest rates [10]_____ up.

Werner: That's true! Well, let's [11]_____ the most of it while it lasts!

4 🎧 **2.4 Listen to these phrases and say in which version – A or B – the speaker sounds more interested and positive.**

1 A ☐ B ☐   5 A ☐ B ☐
2 A ☐ B ☐   6 A ☐ B ☐
3 A ☐ B ☐   7 A ☐ B ☐
4 A ☐ B ☐   8 A ☐ B ☐

Practice

1 🎧 **2.5 Listen to these questions from Ricardo and Werner's conversation. Does the intonation go up (↗) or down (↘) at the end? Mark the correct intonation.**

	↗	↘
1 Can you fill me in with some background to your company?		
2 So, what's your position in the project?		
3 Are you aiming to stay in your present premises?		
4 You're part of a larger group, aren't you?		
5 Is that in line with your plans?		
6 And how does the market look to you at the moment?		
7 How do you see things panning out in the near future?		

2 🎧 **2.6 Listen again and repeat each of the above sentences, concentrating on phrasing and intonation.**

3 What could you say in the following situations?

1 A client has been asking you a lot of questions about your job. You feel you have been talking too much and not learning enough about your client. You want to encourage him/her to talk about his/her job.

2 You want to encourage a client to tell you more about the history of his/her company.

3 A client has told you a bit about his/her job, but you don't really understand what he/she actually does or what the job involves.

4 You want to encourage a client to talk about his/her company's plans for the future.

5 You'd like to know a client's opinion about the business climate for the next twelve months.

6 You want to establish if your ideas about the deadlines for a project are the same as your client's.

4 Complete the sentences using the verbs from the box in the present continuous.

take	expand	aim	look	bring	rise	come	work

1 The company _____ into new markets in the Far East next year.

2 We _____ out updated versions of all our main software in the immediate future.

3 A completely redesigned product range _____ out in the spring.

4 I _____ over as Senior Project Manager shortly.

5 At the moment, we _____ on an assignment for the government.

6 Sales of this product _____ rapidly.

7 We _____ into new possibilities in South America.

8 We _____ for a growth rate of 5% over the next twelve months.

5 **Use the cards on page 47 of the Resources section. If possible, work with a partner. For each situation (1–5), one person takes card A and the other takes card B. Make up a dialogue using the information on the card and the language you have practised in the unit. If you are working alone, imagine what you might say for both cards.**

Example **Situation 1**

A So, Mr Tagana, can you fill me in with some more background to your company?

B Well, we're a very young, dynamic company, established ten years ago. We've expanded rapidly and are currently looking for new markets in ...

6 **Look at page 47 of the Resources section. Practise what you could say in these business situations.**

Consolidation

1 **In your country and culture, can you think of any 'rules' for making conversation? Here are some examples of 'rules' that exist in various cultures. Are any of them true for your culture?**

- We would never interrupt a client.
- It is not considered polite to talk about yourself.
- We don't like talking about the future.
- We would never disagree with someone of a higher status.
- It is not considered polite to ask too much about your client.
- We would always offer someone food or drink before talking business.
- Silence in a conversation is very bad.
- We always exchange business cards first.

Make a list of any other 'rules' in your own culture.

2 **Think about situations in which you may have to start conversations in English with clients or colleagues.**

1 Where are these conversations likely to take place? In the workplace / at conferences or trade fairs / in formal meetings / on visits? etc.

2 What kind of thing will you need to talk about? What kind of information will you need to exchange?

3 **Plan an opening conversation with a client or a colleague. What questions will you ask:**

- to find out more about his/her job/role/company?
- to put him/her at ease?
- to extend the conversation?

4 **When you are next in a situation of making conversation, try out your ideas. Afterwards, think about how it went. What would you do differently next time?**

→ NOW TURN TO YOUR LEARNING JOURNAL AND MAKE NOTES ON THIS UNIT.

Reference

Useful phrases

Finding out more

I understand you're in advertising.

I believe you're in software.

Can you fill me in on some background to the project? *

How do you see things panning out over the next twelve months? *

Are you aiming to expand your business?

What's your forecast for the next financial year?

How does the market look to you at the moment?

Turn-taking

How about you? *

That's true.

Is that in line with your plans?

Broadly in line, yes.

That mirrors our own experience.

Vocabulary

Talking about your company

premises

revenue

site

spend (*noun*)

to be stuck in your ways

turnaround time

well-established

Talking about company plans

cautiously

to diversify

finalize

to look into

to make the most of something

outlook

to oversee

to pan out

to predict

to take over

unforeseen

Talking about trends

buoyant

to creep up

to drop

to even out

to nosedive

to plummet

to rocket

sluggish

steadily

* informal

Study suggestion	It is very useful to build a list of words for describing upward and downward trends, as these are very common in business discussions. Some words are used as verbs, nouns and/or adjectives and adverbs, so it's helpful to record them in a table with examples:		

	verb	noun	adjective/adverb
increase	Sales have increased.	There's been an increase in sales.	We've noted increasing European sales. Our new range is becoming increasingly popular.
nosedive	The market has nosedived.	They recorded a nosedive in the last quarter.	—

Review

Skills

1 Open questions usually begin with a question word, e.g. *What, When, How,* etc. Why are they a good way of making conversation?

2 Think about typical business situations. In what order might you introduce these topics when making conversation?

☐ The general business climate

☐ The other person's company

☐ The forecast for the future of the company

☐ The other person's company products

☐ The details of the other person's job-role.

Useful phrases: keeping a conversation going

Correct the mistakes in the following.

1 Can you fill me up about the background to the project?

2 So what exactly your role is?

3 You merged with CDG last year, do you?

4 Are you aiming to go up your market share?

5 So, how do you see things panning up this year?

6 Is that on the line of your ideas?

7 So, where do you see the market at the moment?

Vocabulary

1 **Put the verbs and expressions for talking about the business climate and possible future trends in the correct category.**

| rise   fall   pick up   be steady   drop   be stable |
| even out   be sluggish   rocket   plummet   creep up |
| nosedive   increase   decrease   be buoyant |

Going up quickly	• _____	**Going down**	• _____
Going up	• _____		• _____
	• _____		• _____
	• _____	**Going down quickly**	
	• _____		• _____
Not moving *optimistic*	• _____		• _____
neutral	• _____		
neutral	• _____		
neutral	• _____		
pessimistic	• _____		

2 **Practise using the words and expressions from Exercise 1 in sentences. Talk about:**

● the market   ● sales   ● borrowing

● interest rates   ● business confidence

Example Business confidence seems to be buoyant at the moment.

Pronunciation

🎧 **2.1 Listen to the dialogues in audio 2.1 again. Take each part and repeat what the person says. Focus on the stress and intonation in the questions and sentences.**

UNIT 3

Building rapport

THIS UNIT LOOKS AT:

■ building a conversation
■ asking about family and interests
■ talking about other personal topics
■ dealing with misunderstandings

Context

1 **Look at this list of conversation topics.**

● Asking about family: relationship/partner/spouse/children/parents
● Talking about interests: hobbies/music/sports/leisure activities
● Asking about where a person lives: house/apartment, etc.
● Asking about where a person lives: country/city/town, etc.
● Complimenting someone on their clothes/hair/jewellery, etc.
● Talking about your salary
● Talking about relationships at work
● Talking about travel and holidays

a **Which of these topics do you think you might use with the following people? Rate the topics on a scale of 1 to 5, where 1 is 'safe' and 5 is 'risky'.**

a a client   c a superior   e a project partner

b a colleague   d a subordinate   f someone of the opposite gender

b **In what circumstances might you talk about each topic?**

2 **Think about the following questions.**

1 In your country and place of work, which of the topics above is it normal to talk about?

2 Are there any topics which you would never discuss?

3 Developing a working relationship often involves sharing some personal information. What questions might you use to open a conversation on any of the above topics?

Presentation

Michelle and Frank work in two different branches of the same company. They are going to be working on the same project and are both attending an induction session for the new project. They are talking during a coffee break.

Personal details

I ⌒ **3.1 Listen to the conversation between Michelle and Frank. In each of these statements, underline the correct answer.**

1 Frank *works / doesn't work* in New York.

2 Frank *has worked / hasn't worked* for the company for more than two years.

3 Frank knew Graham Robson in *New York / London*.

4 Michelle *was / wasn't* Graham's team leader.

5 Michelle has a *high / low* opinion of Graham.

6 Frank has known Graham for a *long / short* time.

2 ⌒ **3.1 Listen to the conversation again. Complete the sentences.**

1 It sounds _____ , doesn't it?

2 Mm, great, and it's _____ to meet the rest of the project team.

3 Yes, it is ... _____ with the New York office long, Frank?

4 Oh really? So _____ Graham Robson, then?

5 Yes, very well – he's an old friend. _____ ?

6 Oh, no, _____ how do you know Graham?

7 Yeah, Graham and I _____ . Small world, eh?

Awkward topics

3 ⌒ **3.2 Listen to the rest of Michelle and Frank's conversation. Answer these questions.**

1 What questions does Frank ask to find out more about Michelle?

2 What information does he discover about Michelle?

3 Which question is probably too personal?

4 How does Michelle respond to the question?

5 How does Frank recover the conversation?

6 How does Frank bring the conversation to an end?

> **Tip** Be careful! Complimenting another person on their dress, hair, jewellery, style, etc. can be very personal and intimate. In western culture, it is mainly done between women.

HARROW COLLEGE
HH Learning Centre
Lowlands Road, Harrow
Middx HA1 3AQ
020 8909 6520

Dealing with misunderstandings

4 ⌒ **3.3 In the conversation, there are three occasions when Frank and Michelle misunderstand each other. Frank recovers the conversation by making clear what he meant to say. Listen to the extracts again and underline the words that are stressed.**

1 Oh, no, I meant how do you know Graham?

2 No, I said 'I'd like to live there.' You know, it's one of my dreams.

3 Oh, I see, sorry. I thought, you know, when you said the two of us, you meant ...

5 🎧 **3.4 Listen to these six dialogues. What are they about? Write the number of each conversation next to a topic. Write any words which give you a clue about the topic area.**

- ☐ leisure activities _____
- ☐ complimenting _____
- ☐ home _____
- ☐ holidays and travel _____
- ☐ interests _____
- ☐ family _____

6 🎧 **3.4 Listen to the dialogues again. Underline the words you think are stressed in the opening questions. Do the questions go up or down at the end?**

Tip Normally, open questions (starting with a question word, e.g. *Where do you ...?*) go down at the end and closed questions (starting with an auxiliary verb, e.g. *Do you ...?*) go up. Be careful – there are several exceptions to this rule.

	↗	↘
1 Did you get them over here?		
2 Do you play, Stanislav?		
3 So, have you got any family, Pablo?		
4 Have you been able to get away for a break this year, Kurt?		
5 How do you normally spend your weekends, Kate?		
6 Whereabouts in Zurich do you live, Rolf?		

Practice 1 **Read these dialogues. Write the full sentence or question using the correct form of the words given.**

Example ▲ When/ you/ join/ company / Franz?

When did you join the company, Franz?

➕ Three years ago in July.

1 ▲ How / you / usually / spend / weekend?

➕ I like to play a round of golf when I can.

2 ▲ Whereabouts / you / base / Georges?

➕ I'm living and working in Munich at the moment.

3 ▲ I / admire / your tie / Ricardo.

➕ Oh, do you like it? I thought I'd wear something bright today!

4 ▲ Do you know Milan, Sally?

➕ No / but / I / really / like / go / there / some day.

5 ▲ you / able / get away / holiday / this year / Andrea?

➕ Yes, we went to Barbados for a couple of weeks in the spring.

6 ▲ And are you still in New York, Michael?

➕ No / I / mean / I / be / there / last year / not this year.

7 ▲ How/ you / know/ Petra Jacobson?

➕ Oh, we worked together a couple of years back.

2 Make sentences with *must* for the following situations.

Example   You think your colleague knows Bridget Nielson, an old friend of yours.
              You must know Bridget Nielson, then.

1   You meet a client at the airport. He looks very tired.
2   You tell a colleague you think she is very well organized.
3   You want to say that your client misses her family.
4   You tell a colleague you think his situation has been difficult.
5   At a conference, someone has mistaken you for another person.
6   You think your client has enjoyed their holiday.

3 🎧 **3.5 Look at the stress and intonation patterns of these sentences and questions. Listen to them and repeat each one, copying the pronunciation.**

1   It <u>sounds</u> ex<u>cit</u>ing, <u>doesn't</u> it?   ↘
2   Have you <u>been</u> with the <u>New</u> <u>York</u> <u>office</u> <u>long</u>, <u>Frank</u>?   ↗
3   So <u>you</u> must <u>know</u> Graham <u>Robson</u>, <u>then</u>?   ↘
4   And <u>what</u> about <u>you</u>?   ↘
5   Yeah, I <u>guess</u> it <u>must</u> be.   ↘
6   And <u>have</u> you got an a<u>part</u>ment like <u>me</u>?   ↗
7   I <u>guess</u> we'd <u>better</u> be <u>getting</u> <u>back</u>.   ↘

4 Work with a partner and look at the situations on page 48 of the Resources section. What might you say and how might you feel?

Consolidation

1 Think about the following questions.

1   What 'personal' topics of conversation might you talk about with a client?
2   Which topics are potentially safer than others?
3   What aspects of culture and gender do you need to take into consideration when personalizing a conversation?

2 Think about the situations connected with work when you may need to talk in English on a more personal level.

1   Where and when are these conversations likely to take place?
2   Would they be with colleagues, subordinates, line managers or clients?
3   Would there be any gender or cultural considerations to take into account?

3 Plan a personalizing conversation at work.

1   How would you move from work-based topics to more personal topics?
2   What would you like to say about yourself?
3   How would you keep the conversation 'safe'?

4 When you are next in a situation of building rapport, try out your ideas. Afterwards, review how it went. What would you do differently next time?

➡ NOW TURN TO YOUR LEARNING JOURNAL AND MAKE NOTES ON THIS UNIT.

Tip We can use *must* to make an informed guess about someone, e.g. *You must know Graham Robson. He must have good taste.*
For the past, we use *must have* + past participle, e.g. *This report must have taken a lot of time.*

Reference

Useful phrases

You must be Bridget Nielson.

You must have had a difficult time.

You must be exhausted.

How do you normally spend your weekend?

Have you been able to get away this year?

Have you been with the London office long?

How long have you lived in Boston?

Whereabouts are you based?

Have you got any family?

Whereabouts in Milan do you live?

What about you?

So (do) I.

I've been admiring your tie.

I guess we'd better be getting back.

It's a small world.

Vocabulary

Talking about people

to be over something

to compliment (someone on something)

to have good taste

divorced

embarrassment

gender

grown up

intimate

lawyer

partner

risky

subordinate

Talking about places

civilized

to get away

horrendous

outskirts

overlooking

spot

General

pretty (*adverb*)

a round of golf

to take leave

to owe

Study suggestion   You can use the transcripts to focus on stress and intonation in connected speech. English is a stress-timed language. This means that we speak with a regular rhythm and we use stress and intonation to convey special meaning. Practise listening and marking the transcripts with the stressed words and the intonation, up or down, e.g.

▲ I've been ad<u>mir</u>ing your <u>ear</u>rings. ↘ Did you <u>get</u> them over <u>here</u>? ↗

＋ Oh, do you <u>like</u> <u>them</u>? ↗ <u>No</u>, <u>act</u>ually they were a <u>present</u> from my <u>partner</u>. ↘

▲ Mm, <u>he</u> must have <u>good</u> <u>taste</u>. ↘

＋ <u>Well</u>, they were <u>my</u> choice, <u>act</u>ually. ↘

Review

Skills **I Answer these questions.**

1 Think of two different ways of asking someone how long they have worked for a company.

2 How could you ask a person about their leisure interests?

3 What questions can you ask to find out more about where a person lives?

4 What different ways are there of asking another person about their holidays?

5 What question could you ask to change the focus of attention from you to the other person?

6 How could you recover the conversation if you realize you have misunderstood or been misunderstood?

Useful phrases **2 Make appropriate questions or statements for these situations.**

1 Ask a colleague when she joined your company.

2 Ask a colleague how long he has been living in his present apartment.

3 Ask a client if he enjoys sports and what sports he enjoys.

4 Ask a colleague if he has any family.

5 Ask a client how she normally spends her leisure time.

6 Ask a client what she did for her last holiday.

7 Compliment a colleague on his choice of tie.

8 Ask a colleague about his tastes in music.

9 Ask a client if there's anything she does or doesn't like to eat.

Vocabulary **Match the words (1–8) with their definitions (a–h).**

1	pretty	a	feeling uncomfortable about something said
2	compliment	b	very personal
3	embarrassed	c	edges of a town or city
4	risky	d	quite
5	outskirts	e	male or female
6	gender	f	not safe
7	intimate	g	someone you are responsible for
8	subordinate	h	say something nice about someone

Pronunciation **3.4 Listen to audio 3.4 again. Look at the transcript on page 57 and practise the dialogues with a partner. Pay special attention to stress and intonation.**

UNIT 4

Entertaining

THIS UNIT LOOKS AT:

■ inviting

■ accepting and declining invitations

■ recommending and making choices

■ asking for help or advice

■ expressing preferences

■ using humour

Context

1 **If you were entertaining a visitor, where would you take your guest?**

● to the theatre or opera

● to a sports event

● to a restaurant

● to an exhibition

● somewhere else

2 **When would you invite them?**

● before the working day

● during the working day

● after the working day

● at the weekend

3 **Have you had experience of entertaining a business visitor or of being entertained?**

● What was good about the experience?

● What was difficult about the experience?

1 4.1 **Listen to each of these four conversations. Write the number of the conversation next to the correct topic. There may be more than one topic in each conversation.**

Inviting/suggesting/offering   _____

Saying 'Yes' to an invitation (Accepting)   _____

Saying 'No' to an invitation. (Declining)   _____

Asking for help or advice   _____

Expressing a preference   _____

2 4.1 **Listen to parts of each conversation again and write any more useful phrases that you hear in the second column.**

Function	Expression	Host/Guest	Formality
Inviting/ suggesting/ offering	Would you like to go out for a meal?	host	N/I
Accepting	Yes, that would be great.	guest	N/I
Declining	I'm sorry, but I'm not very keen on …	guest	F
Asking for help or advice	What are you having?	guest	N/I
Expressing a preference	If you don't mind, I'd rather …	guest	F

3 a **In the third column, write who you think would use the expression, the host or the guest.**

   b **How formal do you think these expressions are? In the last column, write F (formal) or N/I (neutral/informal) for each expression.**

4 4.2 **Listen to the complete list of phrases. Repeat each phrase with the same pronunciation, stress and intonation.**

Humour **5 a We sometimes use humour to 'break the ice' when we are entertaining a guest. You are going to listen to an amusing story. Before you listen check that you understand the meaning of the following words and phrases.**

a hot-air balloon   a balloonist   to float   to lower   IT
(You) haven't a clue

Tip Be careful. Humour depends on the culture and the situation you are in.

b 🎧 **4.3 Now listen to the joke and then tell it to your partner.**

c Did you find this story funny? Why (not)? In what situations would it be appropriate to tell this joke?

Practice **1 Complete each sentence/question with a verb from the box in the correct form.**

have   wonder   care   recommend   decide   suit   have   be

1 Would you _____ the fish?

2 I _____ if you'd like to go on to a club.

3 I'm sorry, but I _____ not very keen on fish.

4 Yes, a quiet drink in a pub would _____ me very well, thanks.

5 Would you _____ for another drink?

6 I'm not sure what to choose, what are you _____ ?

7 It's late, so I think I _____ better get back to the hotel.

8 _____ you _____ what to drink?

2 🎧 **4.4 We often use expressions with *would* when inviting or talking about preferences. Listen again to these examples of *would* and repeat them.**

1 Would you recommend it?

2 We were wondering if you'd like to join us for a meal.

3 That'd be great.

4 That'd suit me better.

5 If you don't mind, I'd rather go back to my hotel.

6 Would you like some?

3 **Here are some more things you might hear or say when entertaining. Match each phrase (1–10) to its more literal equivalent (a–j).**

1 Can I top you up?

2 I'm afraid I really couldn't manage any more.

3 I'll just take pot luck.

4 Nothing ventured, nothing gained.

5 I'm feeling a bit peckish.

6 I think this is my round.

7 What can I tempt you with?

8 This is on me.

9 Any side orders with that?

10 Who's for pudding?

a I'm paying for everything.

b Would you like an extra small plate of, for example, salad, garlic bread, etc.?

c Would you like me to fill up your glass?

d Would anyone like a dessert?

e What would you like?

f I'll have whatever the waiter brings, even though I'm not sure what it is.

g I'm quite hungry.

h I'm full.

i If you never try anything new, you never benefit.

j It's my turn to buy the drinks.

4 **Use the role cards on page 48 of the Resources section to practise the language of asking and responding to situations of entertaining.**

Consolidation

1 **How do you feel about using humour and telling jokes? Is it a normal thing to do in your culture?**

2 **Imagine an occasion when you might a) entertain a guest and b) be entertained by a business client or colleague. Make notes on what you could say for the stages of:**

● accepting or declining an invitation

● recommending or asking for advice

● using humour to break the ice in a conversation

● inviting and suggesting

● expressing a preference

3 **When you are next in a situation of entertaining or being entertained, try out your ideas. Afterwards, think about how it went. What would you do differently next time?**

➡ NOW TURN TO YOUR LEARNING JOURNAL AND MAKE NOTES ON THIS UNIT.

Reference

Reference	*Useful phrases*	*Vocabulary*

Useful phrases

Inviting

How about going to a Chinese restaurant?

I was wondering if you'd like to go out for a Thai meal.

Would you like to go for a drink?

Do you feel like going out for a meal?

We could go to a French restaurant.

Suggesting and offering

Can I get you something to drink?

Would you care for another drink?

What can I tempt you with?

Can I top you up? *

Responding to invitations and offers

I'm afraid I'm not very hungry.

I'm not very keen on Indian food.

I really couldn't manage any more to eat.

I'd rather not have any alcohol.

If you don't mind, I'd prefer a salad.

That'd be great.

That'd suit me.

Would you recommend it?

I'd better not …

Other useful phrases

It's my round.

to feel peckish *

to take pot luck

This is on me. *

* informal

Vocabulary

Menus

hors d'œuvres

nibbles *

starters

entrées

salads

main course

fish

meat

seafood

vegetarian

side orders

desserts

sweets

puddings (BrE)

afters *

Study suggestion	Build your knowledge of colloquial expressions by writing phrases on cards. You can look at these quickly every day until you are sure of using them correctly. Write the function on one side of the card and the example on the other, e.g. *Offering / What can I tempt you with?*

Review

Skills **How many different ways can you think of for:**

- inviting another person?
- accepting an invitation?
- refusing an invitation?
- breaking the ice?

- recommending something?
- asking for help and advice?
- expressing a preference?

Useful phrases **Complete the sentences using *would* and a word from the box.**

recommend	suit	care for	care to	sooner	be	rather	like to

1 ▲ _____ see a show while you're in New York?

  + Great. That sounds an excellent idea!

2 ▲ Shall we have sandwiches for lunch?

  + Yes, _____ me fine.

3 ▲ Can I top you up?

  + _____ great. This wine's excellent!

4 ▲ _____ the roast beef?

  + Yes, an excellent choice. It's always very good here.

5 ▲ I was wondering if _____ go to a Japanese restaurant this evening?

  + Oh yes. I just love Japanese food!

6 ▲ How about stopping for some lunch? There's a good Chinese restaurant just round the corner.

  + Well, _____ carry on till we've finished this agenda. Maybe we could have some sandwiches sent in?

7 ▲ _____ something else to drink?

  + No, thanks, I'd better not. We've got a long meeting this afternoon!

8 ▲ If you don't mind, _____ not go out this evening. It's been a long day, and I've got a bit of a headache.

  + Of course. No problem. See you tomorrow morning.

Vocabulary **Find twelve words in this wordsearch and use them to complete six phrases from this unit.**

D	R	I	T	W	Y	I	T	R
S	I	W	H	A	T	J	R	E
E	F	O	A	E	G	O	O	C
Y	O	U	T	C	A	N	M	O
O	R	L	I	K	E	T	I	M
C	G	D	O	U	G	E	T	M
B	Z	I	C	T	O	M	E	E
P	A	S	U	I	T	P	C	N
C	A	R	E	W	I	T	H	D

1 What w_ _ _ _ _ you l_ _ _ _?

2 What c_ _ _ I g_ _ _ you?

3 What can I t_ _ _ _ _ you w_ _ _?

4 T_ _ _ _ would s_ _ _ _ me.

5 Would you r_ _ _ _ _ _ _ _ _
  i_ _?

6 Would y_ _ _ c_ _ _ _ for anything else?

Pronunciation 🎧 **4.1 Listen to audio 4.1 again and look at the transcripts. Repeat the conversations with a partner. Pay special attention to stress and intonation.**

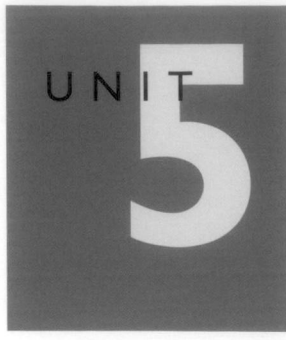

UNIT 5

Making arrangements

THIS UNIT LOOKS AT:

- making suggestions to meet in different situations
- giving reasons for meeting
- agreeing times and places to meet and offering alternatives
- confirming arrangements, numbers and addresses

Context

1 How do you arrange to meet people for business?

- Do you normally make the arrangements yourself?
- Does someone else, for example your PA or the receptionist, make the arrangements for you?
- Do you normally consult your line manager or other colleagues before arranging a business meeting?
- Do you normally make arrangements by phone, e-mail or letter?

2 What do you find difficult about making arrangements in English?

- times and dates
- using the phone
- negotiating the meeting
- clarifying the reason for the meeting and the agenda
- understanding the other person
- offering alternative times and dates

Presentation

Herman Schmidt and Giorgio Cabrisi work in different offices of the same company. Giorgio is a Senior Project Manager and he has been responsible for an important marketing project, which Herman has been helping him with.

Making suggestions to meet

1 🎧 5.1 Listen to the phone call Giorgio makes to Herman. Read the sentences and tick T (true) or F (false).

	T	F
1 Giorgio didn't like Herman's ideas.	☐	☐
2 They are meeting to discuss Giorgio's ideas.	☐	☐
3 They are meeting socially.	☐	☐
4 Herman is free on Friday evening.	☐	☐
5 Four people are going to meet for the meal.	☐	☐
6 They make a definite arrangement to meet on Friday.	☐	☐
7 Herman will pay for the meal.	☐	☐
8 They agree to meet in Bruno's.	☐	☐

> **Tip** If you're not sure if someone is married or not, you can say *partner*, which can mean husband/wife/boyfriend/girlfriend.

2 🎧 5.1 Listen again to the conversation and write the missing words.

1 I wanted to _____ the marketing project.

2 Oh, that's _____ . I've enjoyed working with you.

3 Yes, a meal would be great. So, when _____ ?

4 Well, _____ next week be good for you?

5 Let me just check. Right, I _____ Friday.

6 OK ... _____ if you'd like to bring your partner, and we could make it a foursome.

7 OK, let's say provisionally eight o'clock ... at Bruno's. _____ , by the way.

8 OK, thanks. _____ to confirm, but all being well, we'll see you at eight, then, outside Bruno's.

3 ⬚ 5.2 **Read these sentences. Choose the correct missing word. Then listen to the dialogues and check your answers.**

1 How are you _____ next week?

   a) reserved   b) fixed   c) taken   d) arranged

2 Well, let's _____ it in for now.

   a) pen   b) ink   c) mark   d) pencil

3 We can _____ it up later when you're sure.

   a) make   b) confirm   c) firm   d) define

4 Maybe we can take this discussion _____ over lunch.

   a) later   b) further   c) firmer   d) more

5 Yes, that would be good. When _____ you?

   a) suits   b) fits   c) likes   d) goes for

6 It would be really nice if we could _____ together for a drink or a meal.

   a) meet us   b) go   c) make   d) get

7 Unfortunately, I don't seem to have a clear _____ any evening this week.

   a) window   b) door   c) entry   d) room

4 ⬚ 5.2 **Listen again and write the number of the conversation(s) which:**

a makes a possible but not definite arrangement.

b asks the other person what's best for him/her.

c tells us the suggested date is not possible.

d makes a suggestion to continue the meeting.

e makes a vague arrangement, but nothing specific.

5 ⬚ 5.2 **Listen to the conversations again and answer these questions.**

1 What two dates does Frederico offer Susanna?

2 Why can't Andrea be sure about Thursday?

3 What are the two possible days for dinner?

4 What does Andrew offer?

5 What time, day and place do they confirm?

6 What is the reason for meeting?

7 What expression does Brian use to say he can't meet this week?

Practice   **1 Put these phrases in the right order to make sentences and questions about making arrangements.**

1 if / It would / we could / the project. / to discuss / meet / be good

2 next Monday / be good / Would / for you?

3 two o'clock / Could / next Friday? / you make

4 lunch / How about / for / some time / meeting up / soon?

5 we could / take / you think / this discussion / further / Do / over lunch?

6 next week? / are you / fixed / How

7 need / to get / as soon / We / together / as possible.

8 for you? / When / convenient / would be

2 Complete the sentences using prepositions from the box.

through	in	out	up	together	up	of	back

1 When would you be able to meet _____ ?

2 We'll pencil _____ 10.30 on Monday 4th May.

3 Can I get _____ to you later after I've checked with my boss?

4 Which day were you thinking _____ for our visit?

5 It would be great if we could get _____ to discuss this over lunch.

6 I think it would be best to meet face to face so that we can talk your ideas

_____ .

7 Let's say next Monday evening for dinner, but I'll have to make a few phone calls before I can firm that date _____ .

8 We need a meeting with all the participants to iron _____ the details.

3 Read these phrases used when we make arrangements. Write F (Formal), or N/I (Neutral/Informal) next to each one, depending on the situation when we use them.

1 I was wondering if you'd care to continue this discussion over dinner.

2 Let's get together at the earliest possible date.

3 Next week's out as far as I'm concerned.

4 When would you be able to make a meeting?

5 No can do.

6 What time would suit you best?

7 I was hoping we could make it a bit earlier so I could catch my plane.

8 Could I suggest Tuesday the 23rd as the first possible date?

9 Were you thinking of an all-day session?

10 I'd be really grateful if you could spare me a few minutes this afternoon.

Tip We sometimes use a past continuous form to suggest politeness or distance:
I was wondering if I'd be able to come and talk to you about this face to face.
I was thinking of next Wednesday. Would that suit you?
I was hoping to meet you sometime soon. Would that be possible?

4 a 🎧 5.3 Listen to these sentences and questions. Underline the words and syllables that are stressed.

1 Would any day next week be good for you?

2 I could make Monday afternoon.

3 How are you fixed next week?

4 Maybe we can take this discussion further over lunch.

5 I think we need to get together as soon as we can.

6 Let's pencil it in for now.

7 We can firm it up later when you're sure.

8 I'll see you at three o'clock on Wednesday in the hotel reception.

b 🎧 5.4 Listen and repeat them with the same pronunciation.

5 a There are some differences between British English and American English in the way dates are said and written. Read these dates and times and mark *BrE* (British English) or *AmE* (American English) next to each one.

1 a 06/20/06   b 20/06/06

2 a the second of November   b November second

3 a quarter after four   b a quarter past four

4 a five of seven   b five to seven

5 a at the weekend   b on the weekend

6 a Monday through Friday   b from Monday to Friday

b 5.5 **Listen and check.**

Tip It is better to write out dates to avoid confusion; *12/6* could be 12 June or 6 December, depending on which system is being used!

6 a **Look at these times. Write some of the different ways you can say them.**

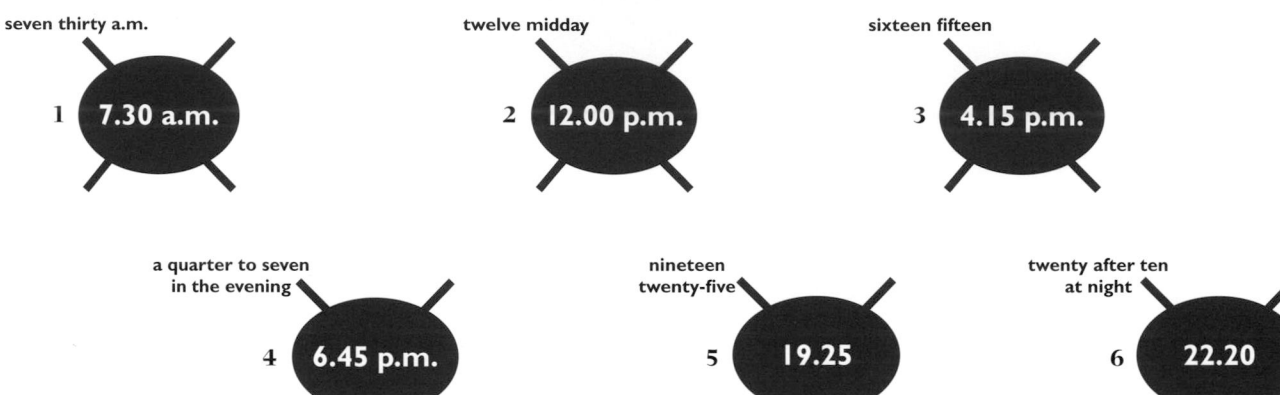

seven thirty a.m.

1 **7.30 a.m.**

twelve midday

2 **12.00 p.m.**

sixteen fifteen

3 **4.15 p.m.**

a quarter to seven in the evening

4 **6.45 p.m.**

nineteen twenty-five

5 **19.25**

twenty after ten at night

6 **22.20**

b 5.6 **Listen and check.**

Tip The 24-hour clock is not used much in American English. Also, times are usually written with a full stop in British English (12.20), but with a colon in American English (12:20).

7 a 5.7 **Listen and write the phone numbers you hear.**

1 _____

2 _____

3 _____

4 _____

5 _____

b 5.7 **Read the numbers aloud and listen again to check.**

8 5.8 **When we make arrangements, we often need to exchange e-mail addresses and websites. Read the following aloud and then listen to check.**

E-mail addresses

1 Annie.Parsons@magicorp.com

2 B.C.Paez@nunez.com.es

3 H.Nasakawa@mbf.sphere.org

4 fsdesouza-saviola@openlink.com.br

Websites

5 www.bex.co.uk

6 www.dti.gov.uk/bestpractice

7 www.MultiplyYourSales.org

8 www.e-motivation.com

9 **Look at the information on page 49 of the Resources section. If you are working with a partner, Student A suggests the time and place, and Student B confirms. If you are working alone, practise different ways of saying and confirming the information.**

Example: A: So we're meeting at Giovanni's on Tuesday, the fourteenth of June. Shall we say twelve forty-five?

B: Yes, that'd be fine. I'll see you at Giovanni's, then, at twelve forty-five on Tuesday June the fourteenth.

10 **Look at the role cards on page 50 of the Resources section. If you are working with a partner, try to negotiate an outcome which is satisfactory to both parties without being rude. If you are working alone, decide what you would say for both roles. Before you start, check the meaning of the following.**

cold-calling	to contact someone without an appointment, usually by phone, usually to sell something
to put someone off	to delay, postpone or discourage someone
to speed up	to go faster
suspicious	a feeling when you don't trust someone
time-waster	a person who wastes your time

Consolidation

1 **Consider the different situations in your job when you need to make arrangements with other people. Which of these people do you need to make arrangements with?**

- people who manage you
- people who you manage
- colleagues you collaborate with
- project partners
- other companies
- clients/suppliers you have met before
- new clients/suppliers
- cold-calling clients
- high-status/important clients
- contacts at fairs and conferences

2 **Think of a real situation in which you have to make arrangements to meet any of the people above.**

3 **When you are next making an arrangement, try out your ideas. Afterwards, think about how it went. What would you do differently next time?**

➡ NOW TURN TO YOUR LEARNING JOURNAL AND MAKE NOTES ON THIS UNIT.

Reference

Useful phrases

Inviting and suggesting

It would be good if we could meet up some time.

Would Tuesday be good for you?

Would you be free on Friday?

How are you fixed this week?

Maybe we can take this further over dinner.

How about meeting up next week?

Could you make Monday afternoon?

I'd like to get together to discuss the proposal.

I was wondering if we could meet.

Could I suggest Monday?

Responding to invitations and suggestions

Thanks for getting back to me.

I could make Tuesday.

I don't have a window this week.

Let me just check my diary.

When suits you?

Next week is out, I'm afraid. *

No can do. *

What time would suit you best?

Were you thinking of this week?

When would be convenient for you?

Confirming times and places

I'll see you at … (time) (day/date) (place)

So, that's … (time) (day/date) (place)

* informal

Vocabulary

cold-calling

promptly

slight

suspicious

time-waster *

to firm something up

to iron something out

to meet up

to pencil something in

to put someone in the picture

to put someone off

to speed up

to talk something through

Study suggestion   In normal speech, we join words together and drop letters. This is why non-native speakers often say they don't understand. It's good practice to look at a transcript while you are listening and to mark the words in the sentence that are joined together. Then you can practise saying the sentence in the same way, e.g. *Would any day nex week be goo fo you?*

Review

Skills **Think of six different ways of making a suggestion to meet.**

1 When might you use each of these suggestions?

2 When might you use a form of the past continuous to make an arrangement?

Useful phrases **Match each beginning (1–10) with an ending (a–j) to make a correct suggestion or response.**

1 How about	a	can take this further over lunch?
2 What time would	b	convenient for you?
3 Maybe we	c	get together with you to talk it through.
4 I was	d	free tomorrow afternoon?
5 When would be	e	meeting up some time soon?
6 I'd like to	f	fixed next week?
7 Could you	g	wondering if we could meet on Wednesday morning?
8 Would you be	h	thinking of early or late morning?
9 How are you	i	suit you best?
10 Were you	j	make ten o'clock next Friday?

Vocabulary **Five of these sentences are correct. Tick (✔) them. In the other five, correct the prepositions.**

1 I didn't want to meet her for lunch, so I put her off.

2 We arranged a meeting to iron in some of the problems.

3 Maybe we can meet on to discuss this further?

4 When would be convenient to you?

5 We can pencil in next Friday for the moment.

6 I wonder if there's any way of speeding up the schedule.

7 Thanks for getting by to me.

8 It would be good if we could talk this through face to face.

9 I can firm up the date for the meeting now.

10 I'd like to take this further through dinner.

Pronunciation 5.2 **Look at the transcripts for audio 5.2 and listen to the dialogues again. Repeat the conversations with a partner. Pay special attention to stress and intonation.**

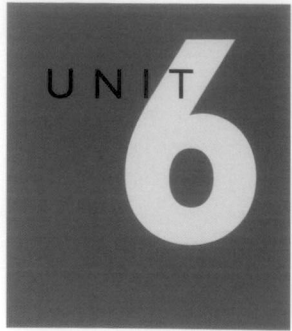

UNIT 6

Leave-taking

THIS UNIT LOOKS AT:

- saying you have to leave
- summarizing at the end of a meeting
- thanking and expressing appreciation
- making plans to follow up

Context

1 **Consider when you might have to leave an appointment or meeting. Which of the following situations might be applicable for you? What would you normally say and do, e.g. promise to call, shake hands, etc.?**

- At a conference or trade fair
- Over drinks at a bar
- Over lunch or dinner
- At a club
- At a sporting event with clients or colleagues
- Visiting a client
- Hosting a client
- Going out with colleagues
- Meeting to discuss business
- Meeting professional associates

2 **What do you find most difficult about leave-taking? Make a note of some of the problems you have encountered.**

Presentation

Anna Gerard has been visiting her company's finance director, Bruce Michaels, to discuss financial arrangements for a new project. They are just finishing lunch.

1 ∩ 6.1 Look at these steps in ending a meeting. Put the steps in the order you think they should happen. Then listen to Anna and Bruce's conversation and check the order.

|6| Anna thanks Bruce and expresses her appreciation.

|☐| Bruce agrees to end the conversation and expresses his concern that Anna catches her plane.

|☐| Bruce summarizes what he has agreed to do.

|☐| Anna asks if there's any unfinished business.

|☐| Anna summarizes what she has agreed to do.

|1| Anna says she has to leave.

2 ∩ 6.1 Listen to the conversation again. Complete the missing words.

1 I'm sorry, but _____ .

2 Can we _____ ?

3 Yes, I'd _____ if I don't want to get caught up in traffic.

4 So, have we _____ everything we need to?

5 I think so. _____ what we've agreed.

6 Right. _____ produce our modified projection before the end of this month.

7 Yes, _____ by Friday the 29th at the latest, after I've met with the technical team.

8 I really appreciate your hospitality and _____ . It's been great.

3 ∩ 6.2 Listen to the rest of Anna and Bruce's conversation and think about the following.

1 How does Anna express her thanks and appreciation?

2 How does Bruce respond?

3 How does Anna repeat her need to leave?

4 How do they agree to follow up the meeting?

4 🎧 **6.3 We use a falling intonation to express certainty. Listen to these phrases and notice how the intonation falls on the final stress. Repeat the phrases with the same intonation.**

1 I really <u>must</u> be <u>going</u>. ↘
2 Can we <u>leave</u> it <u>there</u>? ↘
3 Let's just <u>recap</u> on <u>what</u> we've ag<u>reed</u>. ↘
4 I'll <u>get</u> that to you by <u>Friday</u>. ↘
5 <u>Thanks</u> for <u>everything</u>. ↘
6 It's been <u>great</u>. ↘
7 I'll <u>be</u> in <u>touch</u>. ↘

5 🎧 **6.4 Here are some more common phrases we use when leave-taking. Listen to each sentence and write it in the correct column according to its function.**

Saying you have to leave	Summarizing	Expressing thanks and appreciation	Following up
Can we leave it there for now?			

I **Write full sentences using the following words.**

Example   Thanks / coming / short notice
           Thanks for coming at such short notice.

1 must / going
2 must / tracks
3 leave / there?
4 recap / meeting / so far
5 get / you / end of the week
6 appreciate / done / for me
7 be / touch / soon as possible

2 **We often use expressions with *get* when leave-taking. Put the words in the correct order in these sentences.**

1 Friday. / you / get / to / I'll / by / that

2 get / on / in / I'll / Monday. / touch

3 I'll / done / end / get / by / week. / the / of / the / that

4 you / get / phone / when / I / back. / I'll

5 for / drawn / get / We'll / a contract / you. / up

6 get / the figures / you. / sent / to / I'll

7 I / soon / going / as / as / must / possible. / get

3 🎧 **6.5 Listen to what each person says and write the number beside the best response below.**

☐ a Yes, let's just recap. So, I'm going to call our suppliers ...

1 b Great ... and I'll check those figures again and fax them through tomorrow.

☐ c Yes ... or you can text me. You've got my mobile number.

☐ d No problem. It's been a real pleasure!

☐ e Yes, of course. You mustn't miss your flight.

☐ f I'm glad it's been useful. I'm really looking forward to working together.

4 a Look at the red cards on page 51 of the Resources section and practise making appropriate sentences for leave-taking. Write a correct ending to each sentence using a 'leave-taking' phrase.

b Match the blue cards with the red cards to make suitable endings. Are they the same as the ideas you wrote?

5 Look at the role cards on page 52 in the Resources section. Work with a partner.

Consolidation

1 Think of a situation with a business client when you might have to take your leave. Prepare what you might say in the situation. Think about which of the four stages of leave-taking that we have looked at would be applicable to the situation:

- Saying you have to leave
- Summarizing
- Expressing appreciation and thanks
- Making plans to follow-up

2 When you are next in a leave-taking situation, try out your ideas. Afterwards, think about how it went. What would you do differently next time?

➡ NOW TURN TO YOUR LEARNING JOURNAL AND MAKE NOTES ON THIS UNIT.

Reference

Useful phrases

Ending a meeting

Can we draw it to a close?

Can we leave it there?

I'd better get going.

I must be going.

I must be making tracks. *

Summarizing

Let's just recap.

To sum up, ...

Can we go over it once again?

Expressing thanks and appreciation

I really appreciate all you've done for me.

Thanks for being so helpful/co-operative.

Thanks for making us feel so welcome.

It's been really useful.

I've found our time together really helpful.

Making plans to follow up

I'll get/be in touch.

I'll get that to you by ...

I'll get (something done) by...

* informal

Vocabulary

at short notice

to collaborate

collaboration

deadline

to draw up

to finalize

to get caught up

hospitality

to make tracks

minutes

projection

to recap

to text

Study suggestion   It helps to practise what to say if you can take one part in the conversation. In the dialogues, play the CD part of one person. Then stop the CD and try to say the other person's part. Then listen to the CD to compare. You can use the transcript at first, but try to memorize your part of the dialogue.

Review

🎧 **6.6 Listen to some of the things people say when they are preparing to leave a meeting. Below are four categories involved in leave-taking. Match each statement you hear to a category.**

a Saying you have to leave

b Summarizing at the end of a meeting

c Thanking and expressing appreciation

d Making plans to follow up

Useful phrases **Complete these phrases.**

1 I'm afr _ _ _   I'll ha _ _   to g _ _   going n _ _ .

2 Tha _ _ _   so mu _ _   for every_ _ _ _ _   you've do _ _ .

3 We ne _ _   to ju _ _   go ov _ _   what we' _ _   agreed.

4 I'll pho _ _   you   _ _   soon   _ _   I g _ _   back to the of _ _ _ _ .

5 I appr _ _ _ _ _ _   all the tro _ _ _ _   you've go _ _   to.

6 So, ha _ _   we more or   _ _ _ _   fina _ _ _ _ _   everything we n _ _ _   to?

Vocabulary **Fill in the puzzle and find the secret word.**

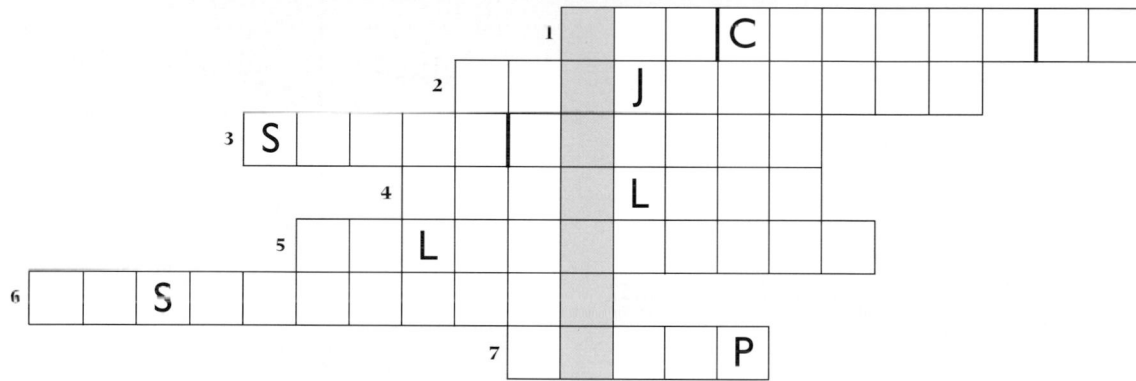

1 'I'd better make tracks. I don't want to _____ in traffic.' (3, 6, 2)

2 A prediction of, for example, results

3 With very little warning (5, 6)

4 The final date for the completion of a project

5 To work together

6 Looking after and welcoming guests

7 To look again at the main points

Secret word

A word often used in leave-taking = _____

Pronunciation 🎧 **6.1, 6.2 Look at audio transcripts 6.1 and 6.2 (page 62). Listen again to the conversation. Read the conversation aloud with a partner, concentrating on your stress and intonation.**

Resources

Note: The material on pages 46–52 may be photocopied for use in class.

Unit 1
Making conversation

do	meet	heard about	My company
before	introduce	... , aren't you?	glad
you're from	nice	colleague	Let me
didn't catch	welcome	repeat	finally
I'm	delighted	pleasure	met
Where ...	role	did you say?	come

Unit 1
What would you say?

1 You meet someone for the first time after communicating with him/her on the phone and by e-mail.

2 You meet a long-term customer after he/she has been on holiday.

3 You bump into some colleagues in a restaurant.

4 Someone offers you their business card, but you realize you haven't got yours with you.

5 You want to ask a client if you can use his/her first name.

6 You realize the other person's English isn't very good and that you need to speak slower.

from *Socialising* by David King © DELTA PUBLISHING 2005

Unit 2
Keeping a conversation going

1A You've only just met and you don't know much about your client's company.

1B You've only just met. Tell your potential client about your company: young / dynamic / looking for new markets / moving into new premises, etc.

2A You don't know what your colleague really does.

2B Tell your colleague about your role: head of design / department of twelve people / working on new government project / looking for new methods of operating, etc.

3A You don't know about the latest developments in your client's company.

3B Tell your supplier about exciting new developments in your company: full order book / expanding into new markets / looking for larger premises / taking on new staff / getting lots of interest in new products, etc.

4A You have just met a colleague from another branch who you will be working with on a project. Outline the project and ask him/her for his/her ideas. Talk about: future meetings, deadlines, how you'll exchange ideas, etc.

4B You have just met a colleague from another branch who you will be working with on a project. Listen as he/she outlines the project. Ask for more details and add your own ideas.

5A Ask your partner what he/she thinks about the business situation and future prospects.

5B Tell your partner about the present business situation and future outlook: has been sluggish / picking up / rise in orders / interest from new markets / interest rates stable / world situation uncertain, etc.

Unit 2
What would you say?

1 You are talking to a new client, but you are expecting an important call on your mobile phone. Your phone rings, interrupting your conversation with your client.

2 You are at a business function. You were talking to someone, but were called away to take an urgent phone call. You have rejoined the person you were talking to.

3 You are at a business function and talking to a possible client. While you are talking, someone else you know comes over to join you.

4 You are at a business function talking to an associate. You have just seen someone you know and who you need to talk to.

Unit 3

What would you say?

1 A visiting client is staying in your town for the weekend. You want to find some common interests so that you can invite him/her to spend some time with you.

2 You find yourself talking to the boss of your company at an office drinks party. The boss is of the opposite gender to you.

3 You are going to work on a new project with a male colleague from another country. He visits your office. You haven't met before. You are talking to him in the coffee break.

4 You try to make conversation about holidays with a visiting client.

5 A line manager of the opposite gender pays you a compliment on the way you are dressed.

6 A visiting client tells you he must phone home urgently on a family matter.

7 You are talking to a female colleague and you find out that her husband has recently died.

8 A colleague of yours wants to talk about one of his/her managers whom he/she doesn't like.

Unit 4

Inviting and responding

A1 Invite B to a nightclub. Use ... *wondering if* ...	**B1** Refuse A's invitation, saying you are too tired.
A2 Ask B what he/she wants to drink.	**B2** Say you don't want alcohol, you'll just have a glass of water.
A3 Ask B if he/she's feeling hungry. Invite him/her for an Indian meal.	**B3** You're feeling quite hungry, but don't like spicy food. Suggest an alternative.
A4 You are in a bar, and B's glass is empty.	**B4** Say you think it's your turn to buy the drinks and ask A what he/she wants.
A5 Say what you prefer to eat. Ask for advice.	**B5** Listen to what A would prefer to eat. Recommend something.
A6 You need to 'break the ice' with B. Say something amusing.	**B6** Listen to A's joke. Tell A another joke.

from *Socialising* by David King © DELTA PUBLISHING 2005

Unit 5

Making and confirming arrangements

1 You have decided to meet at Giovanni's restaurant for lunch on Tuesday 14th June. Suggest a time. Confirm the arrangement.

2 Your colleague suggests meeting for a drink after work on Friday of this week. You're not sure if you can make it. Ask him/her for more details – what time, when, how long for, etc. Finally, confirm a time and place

3 A known and valued client is in town and would like to meet you this evening. He/She doesn't know any good restaurants. Suggest a time and a place. Confirm the arrangement.

4 A business associate would like to take you out for a meal to thank you for your good work on a recent project. Unfortunately, you will be out of the country for the next two weeks. Negotiate a time, date and place which is convenient for you both. Finally, confirm the arrangement.

5 Your boss wants to take you and your partner out to a new Chinese restaurant just opened in town a week on Saturday. Unfortunately, you don't like Chinese food. Try to negotiate an alternative location. Finally, confirm the arrangement.

6 Think of a situation you might actually find yourself in at work where you have to make an arrangement to meet someone socially. Practise making suggestions about time, date and place, and confirming the arrangement.

A1 At a conference

You have met a potential client for your product. You want to develop the contact over dinner. Invite B and try to persuade him/her to join you.

B1 At a conference

You have been talking to A about his/her products, but you don't want to continue the discussion. Refuse the invitation politely, but suggest another time.

A2 Talking to your boss

You urgently want half an hour with B (your boss) to discuss a problem concerning another member of staff.

B2 Talking to your boss

You are A's boss. You are very busy and don't want to hear about A's problem.

A3 Cold-calling

Your company has a new product. You want to arrange to visit B to tell him/her about it face to face.

B3 Cold-calling

You're not very interested in A's product. Try to put him/her off.

A4 Collaborating on a project

You are working with B on a new project. You've got some ideas on how to speed up the schedule. You need a two-hour meeting with B.

B4 Collaborating on a project

You need to talk to A about the project, but you've got a very busy schedule for the next two weeks, including a five-day trip to New York.

A5 Old colleagues

You are trying to sell a new idea, so you are ringing old contacts. You haven't been in touch with B for three years. Arrange to meet.

B5 Old colleagues

You haven't heard from A for three years. He/She suddenly rings you up, and you are suspicious about his/her reasons.

A6 Support from a government department

Your company needs government support for a new project. Speak to a member of the government department to try to arrange a meeting to discuss the project.

B6 Support from a government department

You work for a government department and you are responsible for liaising with local businesses. You want to co-operate with companies, but you must be careful of time-wasters.

from *Socialising* by David King © DELTA PUBLISHING 2005

Unit 6
Practising leave-taking

It's been ...	Let's just ...
Many thanks ...	I really must ...
I really appreciate ...	I'll be in ...
Can we ...	I'll get ...
I mustn't ...	Can we just go ...

... a real pleasure.	... all your hospitality.
... be making tracks.	... for everything you've done for me.
... leave it there?	... miss my flight.
... over what we've agreed?	... recap, shall we?
... that to you as soon as possible.	... touch very soon.

Unit 6
What would you say?

A1 You are aware that B needs to leave to catch a train. However, you want to make sure you have B's contact details before he/she leaves.

B1 You've just looked at your watch and you realize you must go now if you are going to catch your train. Say politely that you have to leave immediately.

A2 You are finding B very boring. You want to leave, but you don't want to be rude.

B2 You are talking to A about your last project. Tell A about the deadlines, problems, people you worked with, etc. Try to make sure you finish before A leaves.

A3 Before you leave, sum up the meeting. You want to make sure B is going to send you the latest price details of his/her products. You're going to put in an order as soon as you've got the prices.

B3 The meeting has ended. You know A wants the latest prices of your products, but they haven't been published yet. However, you want to make sure A makes a firm order.

A4 You have entertained B as a visitor to your company for the last two days. The restaurant last night was awful. You know that B must go to catch a plane. Say goodbye.

B4 A is an important client. You have been entertained as a visitor to A's company for the last two days. The hotel was very noisy, and the meal last night was awful. Thank A and express your appreciation.

A5 You have been talking to B for half an hour in the bar at a conference. Now you don't think B is going to be a useful contact. Politely, say you must leave, sum up the meeting and thank B for buying the drinks.

B5 You have been talking to A for half an hour in the bar at a conference. You think A is going to be a very useful contact. Try to keep the meeting going.

from *Socialising* by David King © DELTA PUBLISHING 2005

Transcripts and answer keys

Unit 1

Transcripts

1.1

Sean Howe: Sorry, I didn't catch your name.

Henrik Pedersen: It's Pedersen ... Henrik Pedersen.

SH: Hello, Henrik, delighted to meet you. It's really nice to see you here. I'm Sean Howe, the lead designer on this project, and this is my colleague Lisa Stewart, who's responsible for organizing the day.

Lisa Stewart: Welcome to Speedsystems ... and you're from ... which company?

HP: PD Solutions. Here's my card, by the way.

LS: PD Solutions, did you say? Oh yes ... I know. You're based in Stockholm, aren't you?

HP: Very good! You've heard of us, then?

SH: Of course, you're in corporate training, aren't you? Your name's getting around.

HP: Oh, is it? That's nice to know. We've heard a lot about you too and this new software you've just brought out ... very interesting.

SH: Really? What sort of thing are you looking for?

HP: Well, as Senior Project Manager, I'm looking for a system which could speed up our initial planning stages ... you know, present a client with a number of options in the shortest possible turnaround time from concept to draft.

1.2

1 ▲ Hello, I'm Mr Cheng from Shanghai.
  ✦ Good morning, we've often spoken on the phone, but it's great to meet you in person.
  ▲ Yes, I feel we know each other pretty well already.

2 ▲ I don't believe we've been introduced.
  ✦ I'm Jill Anderson, Chief Buyer for Mayfield Productions. And you are ... ?
  ▲ Paola Cilento, from Gianni e Donna, Milan.
  ✦ Sorry, I didn't get your first name – Paola, was it?
  ▲ Yes, Paola, Paola Cilento.
  ✦ Very pleased to meet you.

3 ▲ I'm so glad we've finally met. We've heard so many good things about you.
  ✦ It's a real pleasure to be here.

4 ▲ Good morning, Mr Nakita. I'm delighted you could come. Let me introduce my colleague, Michael Evans.
  ✦ How do you do ... and what's your role in the project?

5 ▲ I'm terribly sorry, I'm sure we've met before, but I can't quite place you.
  ✦ Kate Price from Watership Publishing. We met at last year's conference in Madrid.
  ▲ Of course, nice to see you again.

1.3

1 Pleased to meet you.

2 How do you do?

3 Sorry, I didn't catch your name.

4 I'm so glad you could come.

5 I'm really pleased we've finally met.

6 I'd like to welcome you here today.

1.4

1 Meet you ... Pleased to meet you.

2 Do you do ... How do you do?

3 Catch your name ... I didn't catch your name ... Sorry, I didn't catch your name.

4 You could come ... so glad you could come ... I'm so glad you could come.

5 We've finally met ... I'm really pleased we've finally met.

6 Here today ... to welcome you here today ... I'd like to welcome you here today.

1.5

1 ▲ I work for Oxford International.
  ✦ Oh, really? Which office?

2 ▲ I think you've already got the address of our website, haven't you?
  ✦ No, I haven't actually.

3 ▲ I think we've probably been involved in the same project.
  ✦ Oh, have we? When was that?

4 ▲ Hello, you must be Joachim, am I right?
  ✦ Yes, that's right. Pleased to meet you at last.

5 ▲ We're hoping to expand into Eastern Europe next year.
  ✦ Oh, are you? Tell me more.

6 ▲ I'm sure we've met before, but I can't quite place you.
  ✦ Have we? Maybe we met at the Madrid trade fair last year.

Presentation

1 1 Sean introduces Lisa   2 gives
3 the company's name   4 had heard
5 had heard   6 software   7 a buyer   8 faster

2 1 **It's** Henrik Pedersen.

2 I'm Sean Howe … and **this** is my colleague Lisa Stewart …

3 … who's responsible **for** organizing the day.

4 I know. You're based in Stockholm, **aren't you**?

5 Your name's getting **around**.

6 … and this new software **you've** just brought out.

7 What sort of thing **are** you looking for?

3 2, 4, 5, 10

4 1 spoken on the phone; in person; know each other

2 been introduced; didn't get; was it?

3 we've finally met

4 Let me introduce my colleague

5 I can't quite place you

Practice

1 1 Hello, my name's Jill Davis and I'm really pleased to meet you.

2 This is Guy Cartier, who works in our Paris office.

3 Let me introduce Jean-Paul Lemond, our Sales Manager.

4 How do you do? What company do you represent?

5 I'm sure we've met before, but I can't quite place you.

6 I'd like to welcome you here today.

7 Sorry, I didn't quite catch what you said.

8 I'm so pleased you could come.

9 Sorry, but could you repeat that for me?

10 I'm so pleased to have finally met you.

2 1 isn't it?   2 don't you?   3 haven't you?
4 aren't you?   5 haven't you?   6 didn't you?
7 doesn't she?   8 wouldn't you?

3 1 <u>Pleased</u> to <u>meet</u> you.

2 <u>How</u> do you <u>do</u>?

3 <u>Sorry</u>, I didn't <u>catch</u> your <u>name</u>.

4 I'm <u>so</u> glad you could <u>come</u>.

5 I'm <u>really</u> <u>pleased</u> we've <u>finally</u> <u>met</u>.

6 I'd like to <u>welcome</u> you <u>here</u> to<u>day</u>.

6 *Suggested answers*

1 It's really nice to finally meet you in person.

2 Hello, nice to see you again. Did you have a good break?

3 Hello. What a surprise to see you here! Are you enjoying your meal?

4 Thanks. I'm afraid I haven't got my card with me, but I'll send it to you straightaway. Here's my email address, by the way.

5 Do you mind if I call you (Ana), by the way?

6 Sorry, I think I'm probably going too fast. Shall I repeat that more slowly?

Review

Useful phrases

1 d   2 a   3 f   4 b   5 c   6 e

Vocabulary

1 out   2 around   3 about   4 of   5 in   6 up
7 around   8 out

Pronunciation

Suggested answers

1 ▲ I <u>work</u> for <u>Ox</u>ford Inter<u>na</u>tional. ↘

   ✛ Oh, <u>real</u>ly? ↗↘ Which <u>off</u>ice? ↘

2 ▲ I <u>think</u> you've already <u>got</u> the ad<u>dress</u> of our <u>web</u>site, <u>haven</u>'t you? ↘

   ✛ <u>No</u>, I <u>haven</u>'t, <u>actu</u>ally. ↗↘

3 ▲ I <u>think</u> we've <u>prob</u>ably been in<u>volved</u> in the <u>same</u> <u>pro</u>ject. ↗↘

   ✛ Oh, <u>have</u> we? ↗ <u>When</u> was <u>that</u>? ↘

4 ▲ <u>Hell</u>o, you <u>must</u> be <u>Joa</u>chim, am I <u>right</u>? ↗

   ✛ <u>Yes</u>, that's <u>right</u>. ↘ <u>Pleased</u> to <u>meet</u> you at <u>last</u>. ↘

5 ▲ We're <u>hoping</u> to ex<u>pand</u> into <u>Eastern</u> <u>Europe</u> next <u>year</u>. ↘

   ✛ Oh, <u>are</u> you? ↗ <u>Tell</u> me <u>more</u>. ↘

6 ▲ I'm <u>sure</u> we've <u>met</u> be<u>fore</u>, but I <u>can't</u> quite <u>place</u> you. ↘

   ✛ <u>Have</u> we? ↗ <u>May</u>be we <u>met</u> at the Ma<u>drid</u> <u>trade</u> <u>fair</u> last <u>year</u>. ↗↘

Unit 2

Transcripts

2.1

1 ▲ So Piotr, I understand you're an expert in e-learning.

   ✛ Well, e-learning is my area, but like everyone else, I'm learning new things all the time.

2 ▲ How do you see things panning out in the near future?

   ✛ It's a bit difficult to predict the next few months, but we're very confident of continued growth over time.

3 ▲ Are you aiming to stay in your present premises?

   ✛ For the time being, probably. But we're looking at possible sites for expansion.

4 ▲ Our idea is to get phase 1 finished before the end of the year. Is that in line with your plans?

   ✛ Broadly in line, yes. Though it may not be possible to finalize all the details by Christmas.

5 ▲ We're aiming to grow the business by 10% a year. We're looking at that kind of rise in both spend and revenues.

+ Really? That much! Sounds very encouraging.

▲ Yes, going forward we're very optimistic. We're also looking to expand into other related areas.

6 ▲ So, what's your position in the project?

+ My involvement is in terms of overseeing costs and expenses.

▲ I see. So you're the one we need to check with if there's any unforeseen expenditure?

+ Yes, that's right.

2.2

Ricardo: ... yeah, Milan's a great city. Really vibrant and full of life ... So, Werner, can you fill me in with a bit more background to your company?

Werner: Well, as you probably know, we're very well-established. We've been going for over 30 years now. However, that doesn't mean we're stuck in our ways. We're looking to diversify into new products.

R: I see. So presumably that's where you come in.

W: That's right. My role is to look into new possibilities all over Europe.

R: You're part of a larger group, aren't you?

W: Yes, we were taken over by Rodux a couple of years ago. It's meant a big investment in new technology. Essentially, it's transformed the way we do things.

R: Oh really? In what sort of ways?

W: Our office systems, for example. A lot of money's gone into new software, which has revolutionized our turnaround times. It's made us much more ready to respond to our customers and to changes in the market.

R: Sounds really positive ...

2.3

R: Sounds really positive ... and how does the market look to you at the moment?

W: Pretty good. Things were a bit sluggish towards the end of last year, but I guess that's only to be expected, given world events. Orders have been picking up steadily since then, though, and overall, I suppose we're cautiously optimistic. How about you?

R: Yes, that pretty well mirrors our own experience. Mind you, I don't know how long this upward trend'll last, with EU interest rates creeping up.

W: That's true! Well, let's make the most of it while it lasts!

2.4

1 Oh really?

2 Sounds really good.

3 And how about you?

4 That's certainly true!

5 How do you see things panning out this year?

6 And what are your thoughts about the situation?

7 Is that where you come in?

8 Are you planning any major changes in the near future?

2.5

1 Can you fill me in with some background to your company?

2 So, what's your position in the project?

3 Are you aiming to stay in your present premises?

4 You're part of a larger group, aren't you?

5 Is that in line with your plans?

6 And how does the market look to you at the moment?

7 How do you see things panning out in the near future?

2.6

1 to your company? / some background to your company? / Can you fill me in with some background to your company?

2 in the project? / what's your position in the project? / So, what's your position in the project?

3 your present premises? / to stay in your present premises? / Are you aiming to stay in your present premises?

4 aren't you? / a larger group, aren't you? / You're part of a larger group, aren't you?

5 your plans? / in line with your plans? / Is that in line with your plans?

6 at the moment? / look to you at the moment? / And how does the market look to you at the moment?

7 in the near future? / panning out in the near future? / How do you see things panning out in the near future?

Answer key

Context

1 job roles: 1, 6   company plans: 3, 5   a project: 4   the general business situation: 2

2 5, 6, 1, 4, 2, 3

Presentation

1 1 F   2 T   3 F   4 T   5 T   6 F

2 1 fill me in with   2 We've been going
3 where you come in   4 My role is to
5 aren't you   6 It's meant   7 what sort of ways
8 Sounds really

3 1 Sounds   2 look   3 were   4 expected
5 picking   6 suppose   7 mirrors   8 Mind
9 last   10 creeping   11 make

4 1 A   2 B   3 B   4 A   5 A   6 B   7 B   8 A

Practice

1 1 ↗ 2 ↘ 3 ↗ 4 ↗ 5 ↗ 6 ↘ 7 ↘

3 *Suggested answers*

1 So, I understand you're an expert in (human resources).

2 Can you fill me in with some background to your company?

3 So, what exactly is your role?

4 What direction do you see your company taking?

5 How do you see things panning out this year?

6 Is that in line with your plans?

4 1 's/is expanding   2 're/are bringing
3 's/is coming   4 'm/am taking
5 're/are working   6 're/are rising
7 're/are looking   8 're/are aiming

6 *Suggested answers*

1 I'm sorry, would you mind if I just take this call? It's rather urgent.

2 Sorry to leave you like that. Now where were we? I think we were talking about …

3 Oh, hello, (Franz), do you know (Sofia)? Let me introduce you. We were just talking about …

4 Excuse me, there's someone I need to see. Would you mind if I just went over and said hello?

Review

Skills

1 Because they are 'open' questions which encourage people to answer with more than just 'yes' or 'no'.

2 *Suggested answer*

4, 1, 5, 2, 3

Useful phrases

1 Can you fill me **in on** the background to the project?

2 So what exactly **is your role**?

3 You merged with CDG last year, **didn't** you?

4 Are you aiming to **increase** your market share?

5 So, how do you see things panning **out** this year?

6 Is that **in line with** your ideas?

7 So, **how does** the market **look to you** at the moment?

Vocabulary

1 **Going up quickly:** rocket

   Going up: rise, pick up, increase, creep up

   Not moving: *optimistic:* be buoyant
   neutral: be steady, be stable, even out
   pessimistic: be sluggish

   Going down: fall, drop, decrease

   Going down quickly: nosedive, plummet

   Note: *increase, decrease, nosedive* are often used as nouns, e.g. *We've seen an increase / a decrease / a nosedive in sales.*

Unit 3

Transcripts

3.1

Michelle: It sounds exciting, doesn't it?

Frank: Mm, great, and it's good to get a chance to meet the rest of the project team.

M: Yes, it is … have you been with the New York office long, Frank?

F: A couple of years; before that, I was based in London.

M: Oh really? So, you must know Graham Robson, then?

F: Yes, very well – he's an old friend. And what about you?

M: I joined at the beginning of last year.

F: Oh, no, I meant, how do you know Graham?

M: Oh sorry, well, we worked together last year on the Transair project. He was my team leader. He's great – really brilliant to work with!

F: Yeah, Graham and I go back a long way. Small world, eh?

3.2

F: So, I guess you're based in Paris. I'd really like to live there.

M: Oh, did you, when was that?

F: No, I said 'I'd like to live there.' You know, it's one of my dreams.

M: Oh, right! Yes, it's a great city, but oh so expensive.

F: Yeah, I guess it must be … like New York and London. And have you got an apartment like me?

M: A small house, actually. It's big enough for the two of us.

F: Right. And what does your husband do?

M: Well, we're divorced actually. I live with my small daughter.

F: Oh, I see, sorry. I thought, you know, when you said 'the two of us', you meant …

M: No, it's OK. These things happen. I'm over it now.

F: Yeah, still, it's never easy. I just love Paris. It's such a beautiful and civilized place.

M: Yes, it is. When I travel, I realize how lucky I am to live there.

F: Well, I suppose we'd better be getting back.

M: Yep, they'll be waiting to start.

3.3

1 Oh, no, I meant, how do you know Graham?

2 No, I said 'I'd like to live there.' You know, it's one of my dreams.

3 Oh, I see, sorry. I thought, you know, when you said the two of us, you meant …

3.4

1 ▲ I've been admiring your earrings. Did you get them over here?

   ✦ Oh, do you like them? No, actually they were a present from my partner.

   ▲ Mm, he must have good taste.

   ✦ Well, they were my choice, actually.

2 ▲ I hope to get in a round of golf on Saturday. Do you play, Stanislav?

   ✦ Occasionally, but finding the time is a problem.

   ▲ Yes, that's true. I find it's a great stress-buster, though, getting out in the fresh air and hitting a ball around.

   ▲ Yes, I find swimming does the same for me.

3 ▲ So, have you got any family, Pablo?

   ✦ Well, they're grown up now. My boy's at university, studying medicine, and the girl's just qualified as a lawyer. What about you, Daniela?

   ▲ No, I haven't got any children. I live with my partner in Brussels. My job involves so much travelling that it's difficult to think about having kids at the moment.

4 ▲ Have you been able to get away for a break this year, Kurt?

   ✦ Not yet, but next month I'm taking some leave I'm owed.

   ▲ Oh right ... going anywhere nice?

   ✦ I haven't got anything fixed up. To be honest, it'll be nice just to spend a couple of weeks at home.

5 ▲ How do you normally spend your weekends, Kate?

   ✦ Well, if I'm not working or away on business, I like to go to the theatre. I'm a bit of an opera fan.

   ▲ Oh really? So am I. Who's your favourite?

6 ▲ Whereabouts in Zurich do you live, Rolf?

   ✦ We've got an apartment overlooking the lake.

   ▲ Sounds nice.

   ✦ Yes, it's a lovely spot, but the rent's pretty horrendous.

   ▲ Right. So you haven't got your own place, then?

   ✦ No, most places in Switzerland are rented ... not like here.

3.5

1 doesn't it? / exciting, doesn't it? / It sounds exciting, doesn't it?

2 Frank? / long, Frank? / the New York office long, Frank? / Have you been with the New York office long, Frank?

3 then? / Graham Robson, then? / So you must know Graham Robson, then?

4 about you? / And what about you?

5 must be. / Yeah, I guess it must be.

6 like me? / got an apartment like me? / And have you got an apartment like me?

7 getting back. / we'd better be getting back. / I guess we'd better be getting back.

Presentation

1 1 works   2 has worked   3 London   4 wasn't
5 high   6 long

2 1 exciting   2 good to get a chance
3 have you been   4 you must know
5 And what about you   6 I meant
7 go back a long way

3 1 And have you got an apartment like me?
And what does your husband do?

2 She lives in a small house in Paris.
She's divorced with a small daughter.

3 And what does your husband do?

4 She says it's OK and she's over it (the divorce) now.

5 By going back to talking about Paris.

6 By saying they need to get back to the meeting.

4 1 Oh, no, I meant, how do you know Graham?

2 No, I said 'I'd like to live there.' You know, it's one of my dreams.

3 Oh, I see, sorry. I thought, you know, when you said the two of us, you meant ...

5 2: round of golf, stress-buster

1: I've been admiring ...

6: Whereabouts ... do you live?, apartment, rent, own place

4: to get away, a break, leave

5: theatre, opera fan

3: family, grown up, children, partner, kids

6 1 ↗   2 ↘   3 ↗   4 ↗   5 ↘   6 ↘

Practice

1 1 How do you usually spend your/the weekend?

2 Whereabouts are you based, Georges?

3 I've been admiring your tie, Ricardo.

4 No, but I'd really like to go there some day.

5 Have you been able to get away for a / on holiday this year, Andrea?

6 No, I mean(t) I was there last year, not this year.

7 How do you know Petra Jacobson?

2 *Suggested answers*

1 You must be tired after your flight.

2 You must be very well organized.

3 You must be missing your family.

4 It must have been a difficult situation for you.

5 You must have mistaken me for someone else.

6 You must have enjoyed your holiday. / You must have had a good time.

Review

Skills

1 *Suggested answers*

1 When did you join ... ? / How long have you been with ... ?
2 How do you normally spend your weekends?
3 Whereabouts ... ? / What part of ... do you live in? / Have you got an apartment?
4 Have you been able to get away for a break? / Going anywhere nice?
5 What about you?
6 *Apologize and pick up a previous safer topic.*

2 *Suggested answers*

1 When did you join ... ? / How long have you been with ... ?
2 How long have you been living in ... ? / Have you been there long?
3 How do you like to keep fit? / Do you do any sport?
4 And have you got any family?
5 How do normally spend your weekends?
6 Did you go anywhere nice? / How did you spend you last holiday?
7 I've been admiring your tie.
8 What sort of music do you like? / What sort of things do you listen to?
9 Is there anything you prefer not to eat? / Are you vegetarian or anything?

Vocabulary

1 d   2 h   3 a   4 f   5 c   6 e   7 b   8 g

Unit 4

Transcripts

4.1

1 ▲ Would you like to go out for a meal a little later on?
   ✦ Well, that's a really nice thought, but if you don't mind, I'd rather go back to my hotel. I'm really tired after our long day and I've got an early start tomorrow.
   ▲ Of course, I quite understand. You must be exhausted. So, see you tomorrow, then.
   ✦ Yes, see you tomorrow.

2 ▲ Have you got anything on tonight?
   ✦ No, I was just going to go back to the hotel.
   ▲ We were wondering if you'd like to join us for a meal?
   ✦ Oh, right, yes, that would be great.
   ▲ We'd like to take you to this really great Thai restaurant we know.
   ✦ Oh, I'm sorry, but I'm not very keen on Thai food, I'm afraid. You see, I can't eat coconut.
   ▲ Oh, dear, what a pity. We could go to the Chinese in the same street. Would that be OK?
   ✦ Yes, that would suit me better ... sounds great, thanks.

3 ▲ So what can I get you?
   ✦ Mm, I'm not really sure what to have. What are you having?
   ▲ I think I'm going to have a glass of red wine. Would you like some?
   ✦ Mm, no, I'd better not have any alcohol. I've got a long afternoon ahead of me, so just a tonic for me.
   ▲ Ice and lemon in that?
   ✦ Yes, please.

4 ▲ OK? Have you decided what to have?
   ✦ Maybe you could help me? There are one or two things on the menu I'm not sure of. For example, what's 'lemon sole'?
   ▲ It's a white fish ... it's got quite a delicate taste.
   ✦ Sounds nice. Would you recommend it?
   ▲ Yes, it's a good choice. I'll have the same.

4.2

Would you like to go out for a meal?

Have you got anything on tonight?

We were wondering if you'd like to ...

We'd like to take you to ...

We could go to the Chinese ...

What can I get you?

Would you like some?

Yes, that would be great.

Sounds great, thanks.

Sounds nice.

I'm sorry, but I'm not very keen on ...

I'd better not have ...

What are you having?

Maybe you could help me?

Would you recommend it?

If you don't mind, I'd rather ...

That would suit me better.

4.3

A man was in a hot-air balloon, floating over the countryside when he realized he was lost. He saw a man walking his dog in a field below, so he decided to lower the balloon till he was within shouting distance of the dog-walker and ask him for directions.

'Excuse me,' the balloonist shouted, 'but I'm a bit lost, so can you tell me where I am?'

'Yes,' said the dog-walker. 'You're floating in a balloon about twenty metres above a field in the countryside.'

'Do you work with computers in IT?' asked the balloonist.

'Yes, that's right,' replied the dog-walker, 'How did you know?'

'Well, like most people in IT, what you've told me is technically accurate, but it's of no use to me at all!'

'And do you work in management?' asked the dog-walker.

'Yes, that's right,' replied the balloonist, 'How did you know?'

'Well, like most people in management, you don't know where you are, haven't a clue how you got here and have absolutely no idea where you're going!'

4.4

1 recommend it? / Would you recommend it?

2 join us for a meal. / if you'd like to join us for a meal. / We were wondering if you'd like to join us for a meal.

3 great. / That'd be great.

4 suit me better. / That'd suit me better.

5 back to my hotel. / I'd rather go back to my hotel. / If you don't mind, I'd rather go back to my hotel.

6 like some? / Would you like some?

Answer key

Presentation

1 Inviting/suggesting/offering: 1, 2, 3, 4
  Accepting: 2   Declining: 1
  Asking for help or advice: 3, 4
  Expressing a preference: 2

2/3

Function	Expression	Host/Guest	Formality
Inviting/ suggesting/ offering	*Would you like to go out for a meal?*	*host*	*N/I*
	Have you got anything on tonight? *	*host*	*N/I*
	We were wondering if you'd like to ...	host	F
	We'd like to take you to ...	host	*N/I*
	We could go to the Chinese ...	host	*N/I*
	What can I get you?	host	*N/I*
	Would you like some?	host	*N/I*
Accepting	*Yes, that would be great. **	*guest*	*N/I*
	Sounds great, thanks. *	*guest*	*N/I*
	Sounds nice. *	*guest*	*N/I*
Declining	*I'm sorry, but I'm not very keen on ...*	*guest*	*F*
	I'd better not have ...	*guest*	*N/I*
Asking for help or advice	*What are you having?*	*guest*	*N/I*
	Maybe you could help me?	*guest*	*N/I*
	Would you recommend it?	*guest*	*N/I*
Expressing a preference	*If you don't mind, I'd rather...*	*guest*	*F*
	That would suit me better.	*guest*	*N/I*

* These expressions are more informal.

Practice

1 1 recommend   2 was wondering   3 'm   4 suit
   5 care   6 having   7 'd/had   8 Have; decided

3 1 c   2 h   3 f   4 i   5 g   6 j   7 e   8 a   9 b
   10 d

Review

Skills

See the Reference section.

Useful phrases

1 Would you like/care to   2 that would suit
3 That would be   4 Would you recommend
5 you'd care/like to   6 I'd sooner/rather
7 Would you care for   8 I'd rather/sooner

Vocabulary

1 would; like   2 can; get   3 tempt; with
4 That; suit   5 recommend it   6 you care

Unit 5

Transcripts

5.1

Giorgio: Hi, Herman, it's Giorgio here.

Herman: Oh, Giorgio. Hi. How are you?

G: I'm fine. Listen, Herman, I wanted to thank you for all the great work you've done on the marketing project. Your ideas have really made a difference. I'd like to thank you properly over a meal.

H: Oh, that's very nice of you. I've enjoyed working with you. Yes, a meal would be great. So, when were you thinking of?

G: Well, would Friday evening next week be good for you?

H: Let me just check. Right, I could make Friday.

G: OK ... I was wondering if you'd like to bring your partner, and we could make it a foursome.

H: Well, I'd have to check that she's free, but yes, that would be very nice.

G: OK, let's say provisionally eight o'clock at ... Bruno's. This is on me, by the way.

H: OK, thanks. I'll get back to you to confirm, but all being well, we'll see you at eight, then, on Friday outside Bruno's.

G: Great, I'll look forward to it. See you then.

H: Yeah, thanks for ringing. Bye!

5.2

1 ▲ Hi, Susanna. I'd like us to meet up sometime soon.

  ✚ That's good news, Frederico. How are you fixed next week?

  ▲ I could make Wednesday afternoon or Thursday lunch.

2 ▲ I should be free on Thursday, but I'm not 100 per cent sure. There's a slight possibility I'll have to go to Milan. I can tell you tomorrow.

  ✚ OK, Andrea, well, let's pencil it in for now and you can let me know tomorrow.

3 ▲ Are you able to let me know yet about dinner on Tuesday?

  ✚ Well, it should be OK – if not Tuesday, then definitely Wednesday.

  ▲ Either day is OK for me. We can firm it up later when you're sure.

4 ▲ It's been really interesting talking to you. Maybe we can take this discussion further over lunch.

  ✚ That sounds an excellent idea, Andrew.

5 ▲ Ah, Piotr, how about meeting up for coffee one morning soon?

  ✚ Yes, that would be good. When suits you?

  ▲ Tomorrow? Could you make tomorrow at eleven?

  ✚ Yes, I don't see why not.

  ▲ Great, so, that's eleven o'clock tomorrow downstairs in the coffee bar.

6 ▲ It would be really nice if we could get together for a drink or a meal.

  ✚ Yes, wouldn't it? Let's try and make a date.

7 ▲ Hi, Brian. Any chance of us meeting up for a chat over a drink?

  ✚ Sure. Let me just check the diary. Mmm, unfortunately, I don't seem to have a clear window any evening this week.

5.3

1 Would any day next week be good for you?

2 I could make Monday afternoon.

3 How are you fixed next week?

4 Maybe we can take this discussion further over lunch.

5 I think we need to get together as soon as we can.

6 Let's pencil it in for now.

7 We can firm it up later when you're sure.

8 I'll see you at three o'clock on Wednesday in the hotel reception.

5.4

1 be good for you? / any day next week be good for you? / Would any day next week be good for you?

2 Monday afternoon. / I could make Monday afternoon.

3 next week? / How are you fixed next week?

4 further over lunch. / take this discussion further over lunch. / Maybe we can take this discussion further over lunch.

5 as soon as we can. / to get together as soon as we can. / I think we need to get together as soon as we can.

6 for now. / Let's pencil it in for now.

7 when you're sure. / later when you're sure. / We can firm it up later when you're sure.

8 in the hotel reception. / at three o'clock on Wednesday in the hotel reception. / I'll see you at three o'clock on Wednesday in the hotel reception.

5.5

1	a 06/20/06	b	20/06/06
2	a the second of November	b	November second
3	a quarter after four	b	a quarter past four
4	a five of seven	b	five to seven
5	a at the weekend	b	on the weekend
6	a Monday through Friday	b	from Monday to Friday

5.6

1 seven thirty a.m.
   half past seven a.m.
   seven thirty in the morning
   thirty after seven a.m.

2 twelve midday
   twelve noon
   twelve o'clock midday
   twelve hundred hours

3 sixteen fifteen
   four fifteen in the afternoon
   a quarter past four p.m.
   quarter after four

4 a quarter to seven in the evening
   six forty-five p.m.
   quarter of seven in the evening
   eighteen forty-five

5 nineteen twenty-five
   seven twenty-five in the evening
   twenty-five past seven p.m.
   twenty-five after seven in the evening

6 twenty after ten at night
   ten twenty p.m.
   twenty-two twenty
   twenty minutes past ten at night

5.7

1 You can catch me on my mobile on 07798 426367.

2 Yes, have you got my number? It's 674 3013 ... oh and the code, that's 0208.

3 I'd better let you have my cell phone, then you'll be sure to get me ... it's 07802 797240.

4 Do you think you could ring me back when you've firmed up that date? I'm on extension 249, and our company's switchboard is 01782 597228.

5 We're on 020 7924 3822, but you'll need 00 44 if you're ringing from Singapore, and then you drop the first 0 of the local code, of course.

5.8

1 Annie.Parsons@magicorp.com, that's 'Annie' cap A, 'Parsons' cap P, magicorp all one word.

2 B.C.Paez@nunez.com.es, that's capital B, capital C, capital P, then the rest is lower case. 'Paez' is P-A-E-Z, and 'nuñez' is N-U-N-E-Z.

3 H.Nasakawa@mbf.sphere.org, that's cap H dot cap N for 'Nasakawa' at mbf dot sphere – that's S-P-H-E-R-E – dot org.

4 fsdesouza-saviola@openlink.com.br, that's 'fsdesouza' all lower case, no points, hyphen saviola, all lower case.

5 www.bex.co.uk, that's B-E-X, not B-E-C-K-S.

6 www.dti.gov.uk/bestpractice – 'bestpractice' is all one word.

7 www.MultiplyYourSales.org – 'MultiplyYourSales' is all one word, but with cap M, cap Y and cap S.

8 www.e-motivation.com, that's 'e' hyphen 'motivation' dot com.

Answer key

Presentation

1 1 F   2 F   3 T   4 T   5 T   6 F   7 F   8 F

2 1 thank you for all the great work you've done on
2 very nice of you   3 were you thinking of
4 would Friday evening   5 could make
6 I was wondering   7 This is on me
8 I'll get back to you

3 1 b   2 d   3 c   4 b   5 a   6 d   7 a

4 a 2, 3   b 1, 5   c 7   d 4   e 6

5 1 Wednesday afternoon and Thursday lunch.

2 She might have to go to Milan.

3 Tuesday or Wednesday.

4 To continue the discussion over lunch.

5 Eleven o'clock, tomorrow, downstairs in the coffee bar.

6 To have a drink or a meal.

7 I don't seem to have a clear window any evening this week.

Practice

1 1 It would be good if we could meet to discuss the project.

2 Would next Monday be good for you?

3 Could you make two o'clock next Friday?

4 How about meeting up for lunch some time soon?

5 Do you think we could take this discussion further over lunch?

6 How are you fixed next week?

7 We need to get together as soon as possible.

8 When would be convenient for you?

2 1 up   2 in   3 back   4 of   5 together
6 through   7 up   8 out

3 1 F   2 N/I   3 N/I   4 N/I   5 N/I   6 N/I   7 F
8 F   9 N/I   10 F

4 1 Would any day <u>next</u> week be <u>good</u> for you?

2 I could make <u>Mon</u>day after<u>noon</u>.

3 <u>How</u> are you <u>fixed</u> next <u>week</u>?

4 <u>Maybe</u> we can <u>take</u> this dis<u>cussion</u> <u>further</u> over <u>lunch</u>.

5 I <u>think</u> we need to <u>get</u> to<u>geth</u>er as <u>soon</u> as we <u>can</u>.

6 Let's <u>pencil</u> it <u>in</u> for <u>now</u>.

7 We can <u>firm</u> it up <u>later</u> when you're <u>sure</u>.

8 I'll see you at <u>three</u> o'<u>clock</u> on <u>Wed</u>nesday in the <u>hotel</u> re<u>cep</u>tion.

5 1 a AmE   b Br E

2 a BrE   b AmE

3 a AmE   b BrE

4 a AmE   b BrE

5 a BrE   b AmE

6 a AmE   b BrE

6 1 seven thirty a.m.
half past seven a.m.
seven thirty in the morning
thirty after seven a.m.

2 twelve midday
twelve noon
twelve o'clock midday
twelve hundred hours

3 sixteen fifteen
four fifteen in the afternoon
a quarter past four p.m.
quarter after four

4 a quarter to seven in the evening
six forty-five p.m.
quarter of seven in the evening
eighteen forty-five

5 nineteen twenty-five
seven twenty-five in the evening
twenty-five past seven p.m.
twenty-five after seven in the evening

6 twenty after ten at night
ten twenty p.m.
twenty-two twenty
twenty minutes past ten at night

7 1 07798 426367
2 0208 674 3013
3 07802 797240
4 01782 597228 ext. 249
5 00 44 20 7924 3822

Review

Skills

2 See the Tip on page 35.

Useful phrases

1 e   2 i   3 a   4 g   5 b   6 c   7 j   8 d   9 f   10 h

Vocabulary

1 ✔

2 We arranged a meeting to iron **out** some of the problems.

3 Maybe we can meet **up** to discuss this further?

4 When would be convenient **for** you?

5 ✔

6 ✔

7 Thanks for getting **back** to me.

8 ✔

9 ✔

10 I'd like to take this further **over** dinner.

Unit 6

Transcripts

6.1

Anna: I'm sorry, but I really must be going. Can we leave it there?

Bruce: Yes, of course. You mustn't miss your flight. We need to get you to the airport before the rush hour.

A: Yes, I'd better get going if I don't want to get caught up in traffic. So, have we more or less finalized everything we need to?

B: Mm-hm. I think so. Let's just recap on what we've agreed.

A: Right. I'm going to produce our modified projection before the end of this month.

B: With new costings and deadlines?

A: Yes, I'll get that to you by Friday the 29th at the latest, after I've met with the technical team.

B: And we're going to review the financing arrangements in line with your extra costs.

A: Mmm, that's right. So, thanks for everything. I really appreciate your hospitality and everything you've done for me. It's been great.

6.2

B: And we're going to review the financing arrangements in line with your extra costs.

A: That's right. So, thanks for everything. I really appreciate your hospitality and everything you've done for me. It's been great.

B: Our pleasure, we're here to help if we can. Thank you for coming over at such short notice. I'm looking forward to our collaboration.

A: Likewise. Well, I must be making tracks or I'll miss my plane. I'll be in touch as soon as I'm back in the office.

B: Yes, I'll firm up the minutes of this meeting and send them to you. When we've got your modifications, I'll get a draft contract drawn up.

A: Great. Well, thanks again and I'm sure we'll be meeting up before too long.

B: Yes, just ask the waiter to call you a taxi. Have a good flight back.

A: Thanks, bye.

6.3

1 I really must be going.

2 Can we leave it there?

3 Let's just recap on what we've agreed.

4 I'll get that to you by Friday.

5 Thanks for everything.

6 It's been great.

7 I'll be in touch.

6.4

1 Can we leave it there for now?

2 I'll get in touch as soon as I've got the figures.

3 I'm really grateful to you for all you've done.

4 So, can we go over what we've agreed?

5 Well, I'd better be making tracks.

6 I think we need to recap on the situation so far.

7 I'll text you before the end of tomorrow.

8 You've been really helpful.

9 I need to draw things to a close.

10 I'll put this in writing to you.

11 You've made me feel really welcome.

12 Is there anything else we need to finalize before you go?

6.5

1 I'll put this in writing to you as soon as I get back.

2 Thanks so much for all your hospitality.

3 I'm sorry to interrupt, but I really must get going.

4 Thanks for being so co-operative. I've found our time together really helpful.

5 Can we just go over what's been agreed?

6 I'll e-mail our decision as soon as the board have decided.

6.6

1 Thanks so much for all your hospitality.

2 I'll put this in writing to you as soon as I get back.

3 I'm sorry to interrupt, but I really must get going.

4 Thanks for being so co-operative. I've found our time together really helpful.

5 Can we just go over what's been agreed?

6 Is it OK to leave it at that point? I'm a bit concerned about my flight.

7 I'll e-mail our decision as soon as the board have decided.

8 I'm really grateful for everything you've done for me.

Answer key

Presentation

1 6, 2, 5, 3, 4, 1

2 1 I really must be going   2 leave it there   3 better get going   4 more or less finalized   5 Let's just recap on   6 I'm going to   7 I'll get that to you 8 everything you've done for me

3 1 So, thanks for everything. I really appreciate your hospitality and everything you've done for me.

2 Our pleasure, we're here to help if we can. Thank you for coming over at such short notice.

3 Well, I must be making tracks or I'll miss my plane.

4 Anna: I'll be in touch as soon as I'm back in the office.
Bruce: I'll firm up the minutes of this meeting and send them to you. When we've got your modifications, I'll get a draft contract drawn up.

5

Saying you have to leave	Summarizing	Expressing thanks and appreciation	Following up
Can we leave it there for now? Well, I'd better be making tracks. I need to draw things to a close.	So, can we go over what we've agreed? I think we need to recap on the situation so far. Is there anything else we need to finalize before you go?	I'm really grateful to you for all you've done. You've been really helpful. You've made me feel really welcome.	I'll get in touch as soon as I've got the figures. I'll text you before the end of tomorrow. I'll put this in writing to you.

Practice

1 1 I really must be/get going.

2 I (really) must be making tracks.

3 Can we leave it there?

4 Let's recap on the meeting so far.

5 I'll get that to you by/before the end of the week. / I'll get back to you by/before the end of the week.

6 I really appreciate everything you've done for me.

7 I'll be in touch as soon as possible.

2 1 I'll get that to you by Friday.

2 I'll get in touch on Monday.

3 I'll get that done by the end of the week.

4 I'll phone you when I get back.

5 We'll get a contract drawn up for you.

6 I'll get the figures sent to you.

7 I must get going as soon as possible.

3 1 b 2 d 3 e 4 f 5 a 6 c

Review

Skills

a Saying you have to leave: 3, 6

b Summarizing at the end of a meeting: 5

c Thanking and expressing appreciation: 1, 4, 8

d Making plans to follow up: 2, 7

Useful phrases

1 I'm afraid I'll have to get going now.

2 Thanks so much for everything you've done.

3 We need to just go over what we've agreed.

4 I'll phone you as soon as I get back to the office.

5 I appreciate all the trouble you've gone to.

6 So, have we more or less finalized everything we need to?

Vocabulary

1 get caught up   2 projection   3 short notice
4 deadline   5 collaborate   6 hospitality   7 recap
Secret word: goodbye